FAITH

Spencer W. Kimball

Marion G. Romney

Gordon B. Hinckley

Ezra Taft Benson

Mark E. Petersen

Howard W. Hunter

Boyd K. Packer

Marvin J. Ashton

Bruce R. McConkie

L. Tom Perry

J. Thomas Fyans

M. Russell Ballard

Theodore M. Burton

Loren C. Dunn

Rex D. Pinegar

Joseph B. Wirthlin

Gene R. Cook

F. Enzio Busche

Joseph Anderson

FAITH

Deseret Book Company
Salt Lake City, Utah

© 1983 Deseret Book Company
All rights reserved
Printed in the United States of America
ISBN 0-87747-980-1
Library of Congress Card Catalog Number 83-72343

First printing September 1983
Second printing January 1984

CONTENTS

FAITH PRECEDES
THE MIRACLE

President Spencer W. Kimball

Throughout the Church hundreds of thousands of faithful Saints have truly consecrated their lives and their energies to the work of the Lord, secure in the assurance that thereby they please Him.

It is a disappointment, however, to find many others who are not willing to trust the Lord—or to trust in His promise when He says, "Prove me and see." I often wonder why men cannot trust their Lord. He has promised His children every blessing contingent upon their faithfulness, but fickle man places his trust in "the arm of flesh" and sets about to make his own way unaided by Him who could do so much.

The Lord has challenged us: "Prove me . . . if I will not open you the windows of heaven, and pour you out a blessing, that there shall not be room enough to receive it." (Malachi 3:10.)

The prophet Moroni stopped abruptly in his abridging to offer his own inspired comments concerning the matter of faith: "I would show unto the world that faith is things which are hoped for and not seen; wherefore, dispute not because ye see not, for ye receive no witness until after the trial of your faith." (Ether 12:6.)

Father Adam understood this basic principle: "An angel of the Lord appeared unto Adam, saying: Why dost thou offer sacrifices unto the Lord? And Adam said unto him: I know not, save the Lord commanded me." (Moses 5:6.) He showed his unwavering faith—and since the witness and the miracle follow rather than precede the faith, the angel then sought to enlighten him, saying: "This thing is a similitude of the sacrifice of the Only Begotten of the Father." (Moses 5:7.)

In faith we plant the seed, and soon we see the miracle of the blossoming. Men have often misunderstood and have reversed the process. They would have the harvest before the

1

planting, the reward before the service, the miracle before the faith. Even the most demanding labor unions would hardly ask the wages before the labor. But many of us would have the vigor without the observance of the health laws, prosperity through the opened windows of heaven without the payment of our tithes. We would have the close communion with our Father without fasting and praying. We would have rain in due season and peace in the land without observing the Sabbath and keeping the other commandments of the Lord. We would pluck the rose before planting the roots; we would harvest the grain before sowing and cultivating.

If only we could realize, as Moroni writes, that "if there be no faith among the children of men God can do no miracle among them. . . . And neither at any time hath any wrought miracles until after their faith; wherefore they first believed in the Son of God." (Ether 12:12, 18.)

The Lord has made it clear that faith is not developed by miracles. To the scribes and Pharisees who demanded signs without the preliminary faith and works, He said: "An evil and adulterous generation seeketh after a sign." (Matthew 12:39.) In modern-day revelation He has said: "But, behold, faith cometh not by signs, but signs follow those that believe." (D&C 63:9.)

In the early days of the restoration of the Church, Sidney Rigdon did not retain his membership in the kingdom even though he had, with Joseph Smith, witnessed marvelous signs. Had he not participated in the great vision, and had he not been the recipient of many revelations? Yet despite all these manifestations from our Heavenly Father, he did not remain in the kingdom.

Oliver Cowdery saw many signs. He handled the sacred plates; saw John the Baptist; received the higher priesthood from Peter, James, and John; and was the recipient of many great miracles; and yet they could not hold him to the faith.

Amassed evidence in signs and works and miracles failed to touch the stony hearts of the Galilean cities: "Then began he to upbraid the cities wherein most of his mighty works

2

were done, because they repented not: Woe unto thee, Chorazin! woe unto thee, Bethsaida! . . . And thou, Capernaum, which art exalted unto heaven, shalt be brought down to hell: for if the mighty works, which have been done in thee, had been done in Sodom, it would have remained until this day." (Matthew 11:20-21, 23.)

Paul, speaking to the Hebrews, said: "By faith Noah, being warned of God of things not seen as yet, moved with fear, prepared an ark to the saving of his house." (Hebrews 11:7.) As yet there was no evidence of rain and flood, so the people mocked Noah and called him a fool. His preaching fell on deaf ears. His warnings were considered irrational. There was no precedent; never had it been known that a deluge could cover the earth. How foolish to build an ark on dry ground with the sun shining and life moving forward as usual! But time ran out. The ark was finished. The floods came. The disobedient and rebellious were drowned. The miracle of the ark followed the faith manifested in its building.

Paul also wrote concerning the faith of Abraham and Sarah. Of Abraham he said: "By faith Abraham, when he was called to go out into a place which he should after receive for an inheritance, obeyed; and he went out, not knowing whither he went." (Hebrews 11:8.)

Paul said concerning Sarah: "Through faith . . . [she] herself received strength to conceive seed, and was delivered of a child when she was past age, because she judged him faithful who had promised. Therefore sprang there even of one, and him as good as dead, so many as the stars of the sky in multitude, and as the sand which is by the sea shore innumerable." (Hebrews 11:11-12.)

So absurd was it to be told that children could be born of centenarians that even Sarah doubted at first. But the faith of a noble pair prevailed, and the miracle son was born to father multitudes of nations.

Exceeding faith was shown by Abraham when the superhuman test was applied to him. Isaac, his young "child of promise," must now be offered upon the sacrificial altar. It was God's command, but it seemed so contradictory! How could Isaac be the father of an uncountable posterity if in his youth his mortal life was to be terminated? Why should he, Abraham, be called upon to do this revolting deed? It was irreconcilable, impossible! And yet he believed God. His undaunted faith carried him with breaking heart toward Mount Moriah with this young son, who little suspected the agonies through which his father must have been passing. Saddled asses took the party and supplies. The father and the son, carrying the fire and the wood, mounted to the place of sacrifice.

"Behold the fire and the wood," said Isaac, "but where is the lamb for a burnt offering?" What a heavy heart and sad voice it must have been that replied: "My son, God will provide himself a lamb for a burnt offering."

The place was reached, the altar built, the fire kindled, and the lad, now surely knowing, but trusting and believing, was upon the altar. Then the father's raised hand was stopped in midair by a commanding voice: "Lay not thine hand upon the lad. . . . Now I know that thou fearest God, seeing thou hast not withheld thy son, thine only son from me."

As the near-perfect prophet found the ram in the thicket and offered it upon the altar, he heard the voice of God again speaking: "In thy seed shall all the nations of the earth be blessed; because thou hast obeyed my voice." (See Genesis 22.)

This great and noble Abraham—"who against hope believed in hope, that he might become the father of many nations . . . and being not weak in faith, he considered not his own body now dead, when he was about an hundred years old, neither yet the deadness of Sarah's womb:

"He staggered not at the promise of God through unbelief; but was strong in faith, giving glory to God; and being fully persuaded that, what he had promised, he was able also to perform." (Romans 4:18-21.)

Father Abraham and Mother Sarah knew that the promise would be fulfilled. Isaac positively would live to be the

4

father of a numerous posterity. They knew that he would, even though he might need to die. They knew that he could still be raised from the dead to fulfill the promise, and faith here preceded the miracle.

Paul told the Hebrews that by faith the children of Israel "passed through the Red sea as by dry land." (Hebrews 11:29.) The Israelites knew, as did Pharaoh and his hosts, that they were "entangled in the land," shut in by the wilderness. As Pharaoh's trained army approached with all the horses and chariots of Egypt, the escaping multitudes knew full well that they were hemmed in by the marshes, the deserts, and the sea. There was no earthly chance for them to escape the wrath of their pursuers. And in their terror they indicted Moses: "Because there were no graves in Egypt, hast thou taken us away to die in the wilderness? . . . It had been better for us to serve the Egyptians, than that we should die in the wilderness."

No hope on earth for their liberation! What could save them now? The gloating armed forces of Egypt knew that the children of Israel were trapped. Israel knew it only too well. But Moses, their inspired leader with supreme faith, knew that God would not have called them on this exodus only to have them destroyed. He knew that God would provide the escape. He may not at this moment have known just how, but he trusted. He commanded his people: "Fear ye not, stand still, and see the salvation of the Lord, which he will shew to you to day: for the Egyptians whom ye have seen to day, ye shall see them again no more for ever. The Lord shall fight for you."

The mighty warriors pressed on. Hope must have long since died in the breasts of the timid Israelites who knew not faith. Deserts and wilderness and the sea—the uncrossable sea! No boats, no rafts, no bridges, nor time to construct them! Hopelessness, fear, despair must have gripped their hearts.

And then the miracle came. It was born of the faith of their indomitable leader. A cloud hid them from the view of their enemies. A strong east wind blew all the night; the waters were parted; the bed of the sea was dry; and Israel crossed to another world and saw the returning sea envelop and destroy their pursuers. Israel was safe. Faith had been rewarded, and Moses was vindicated. The impossible had happened. An almost superhuman faith had given birth to an unaccountable and mysterious miracle that was to be the theme of the sermons and warnings of Israel and their prophets for centuries. (See Exodus 14.)

Israel was later ready to cross into the Promised Land, the productivity and beauty of which could probably be seen from the higher hills. But how to get there? There were no bridges or ferries across the flooding Jordan. A great prophet, Joshua, received the mind of the Lord and commanded, and another miracle was born of faith.

"And [as] the feet of the priests that bare the ark were dipped in the brim of the water, . . . the waters which came down from above stood and rose up upon an heap . . . and those that came down . . . failed, and were cut off. . . . And all the Israelites passed over on dry ground, until all the people were passed clean over Jordan." (Joshua 3:15-17.)

The elements find control through faith. The wind, the clouds, the heavens obey the voice of faith. It was by and through the faith of Elijah that the drouth that had devastated Israel for three interminable years was finally ended when repentance had come to Israel. The brooks had dried up; rivers had ceased to run; forage had become scarce; and famine was upon the land. A king and his people were begging for relief—a people who had lost themselves in the worship of Baal. At Mount Carmel came the contest of power. At Elijah's command, fire came down from heaven and ignited the sacrifice and shocked the Baal worshipers once more into repentant submission. Miracle followed faith again, and though the heavens were still clear and there was no indication of rain on the parched land, Elijah warned King Ahab: "Prepare thy chariot, and get thee down, that the rain stop thee not." (1 Kings 18:44.)

With his face between his knees as he sat on Carmel, Elijah sent his servant seven times to look toward the sea.

Six times there were cloudless skies and calm sea, but on the seventh he reported: "Behold, there ariseth a little cloud out of the sea, like a man's hand." Soon the heavens were black with clouds, the wind was carrying them to Palestine, and "there was a great rain." A dry, parched land was drenched in moisture, and the miracle of faith had again made good the promises of the Lord. (See 1 Kings 17, 18.)

It was by supreme faith that three Hebrews were delivered from the fiery furnace of their king, Nebuchadnezzar. The king asked his councilors, "Did not we cast three men bound into the midst of the fire?" They answered, "True, O king." He then said, "Lo, I see four men loose, walking in the midst of the fire, and they have no hurt; and the form of the fourth is like the Son of God." Then all the people who had gathered saw the men, "upon whose bodies the fire had no power, nor was an hair of their head singed, neither were their coats changed, nor the smell of fire had passed on them." (See Daniel 3:19-27.)

Now, if you would discount these miracles of the Old Testament, how can you accept the New Testament? You would also have difficulty in accepting Paul, the apostles, and the Lord Jesus Christ, for they verified and documented those miraculous events.

How can these stories of faith be brought into our own lives? Faith is needed as much today as ever before. Little can we see. We know not what the morrow will bring. Accidents, sickness, even death seem to hover over us continually. Little do we know when they might strike.

It takes faith—unseeing faith—for young people to proceed immediately with their family responsibilities in the face of financial uncertainties. It takes faith for the young woman to bear her family instead of accepting employment, especially when the young husband's schooling is to be finished. It takes faith to observe the Sabbath when time and a half can be had working, when profit can be made, when merchandise can be sold. It takes great faith to pay tithes when funds are scarce and demands are great. It takes faith to fast and have family prayers and observe the Word of Wisdom. It takes faith to do home teaching, stake missionary work, and other service, when sacrifice is required. It takes faith to fill full-time missions. But know this: all these are of the planting, while faithful, devout families, spiritual security, peace, and eternal life are the harvest.

Remember that Abraham, Moses, Elijah, and others could not see clearly the end from the beginning. They also walked by faith and without sight.

Remember again that no gates were open; Laban was not drunk; and no earthly hope was justified at the moment Nephi exercised his faith and set out finally to get the plates.

Remember that there were no clouds in the sky, no evidence of rain, and no precedent for the deluge when Noah built the ark according to commandment.

Remember that there was no ram in the thicket when Isaac and his father left for Moriah for the sacrifice.

Remember that though Joshua may have witnessed the miracle of the Red Sea, he could not by mortal means perceive that the flooding Jordan would back up for the exact time needed for the crossing, and then flow again on its way to the Dead Sea. Remember that there were no clouds in the sky nor any hygrometer in his hand when Elijah promised an immediate break in the long extended drouth.

Remember that there were no heavenly beings in Palmyra, on the Susquehanna, or on Cumorah when the soul-hungry Joseph slipped quietly into the grove, knelt in prayer on the river bank, and climbed the slopes of the sacred hill.

And remember that there were no towns and cities, no farms and gardens, no homes and storehouses, no blossoming desert in Utah when the persecuted pioneers crossed the plains.

But know this: Just as undaunted faith has stopped the mouths of lions, made ineffective fiery flames, opened dry corridors through rivers and seas, protected against deluge and drouth, and brought heavenly manifestations at the instance of prophets, so in each of our lives faith can heal the sick, bring comfort to those who mourn, strengthen resolve against temptation, relieve from the bondage of harmful habits, lend the strength to repent and change our lives, and lead to a sure knowledge of the divinity of Jesus Christ. Indomitable faith can help us live the commandments with a willing heart and thereby bring blessings unnumbered, with peace, perfection, and exaltation in the kingdom of God.

THE POWER
OF FAITH

President Marion G. Romney

"Now faith is the substance of things hoped for, the evidence of things not seen." (Hebrews 11:1.)

"Being justified by faith, we have peace with God through our Lord Jesus Christ: by whom also we have access by faith into this grace wherein we stand, and rejoice in hope of the glory of God." (Romans 5:1-2.)

In his preface to the Book of Commandments, the Lord said that one of His purposes in giving Joseph Smith this revelation was "that faith also might increase in the earth." (D&C 1:21.)

The Prophet Joseph Smith named "faith in the Lord Jesus Christ" as the first principle of the gospel.

Blessed is he who, based on a knowledge of the gospel, has unshakable faith in the Lord Jesus Christ. Such a one has for his goal the attainment of eternal life. He has an anchor to his soul, and a motive for action.

1. *The possessor of such a faith has a sound understanding of the purpose of life.*

He knows that God lives. He knows that he himself is a begotten child of God, and that as such he is endowed with the potential eventually to rise to the full stature of his Heavenly Father. And he is intimately acquainted with the plan by which he may do so. Thus fortified, he is not "driven with the wind and tossed" (James 1:6), but stands serene and confident amid the ups and downs of life. Like the Valley of Lemuel, he remains "firm and steadfast, and immovable" (1 Nephi 2:10), his goal fixed by his knowledge of the purpose of life.

2. *The possessor of such faith has a sure test by which to distinguish truth from error.*

He knows that he lives in a day of great conflict between good and evil; that anti-Christs stalk the earth in all lands;

10

that false philosophies and doctrines emanating from the Prince of Darkness are being presented in such an appealing manner as almost to deceive the very elect. All this he knows and more.

He knows that earth was created to be a battleground for the souls of men; that this life is a testing time; that in mortality men must struggle between the two mighty forces of truth and error.

He is strengthened for the conflict by the knowledge that God, his Heavenly Father, has not abandoned him in the struggle, but has put within his reach the knowledge and wisdom upon which he can correctly distinguish good from evil. He knows that such knowledge has been revealed from heaven and that it may be found in the scriptures and in the teachings of the living prophets.

He knows this because he has studied and searched scriptures and has listened to and pondered what the living prophets say. He has also fasted and prayed about the teachings of the scriptures and living prophets. He knows from his own experience that faith comes from searching, hearing, pondering, and praying about the word of God. He knows that he himself has the gift of revelation by which he may not only correctly interpret the scriptures and the teachings of the living prophets, but also properly conduct his own personal affairs.

He is not led astray by false teachings, theories, and philosophies, for he tests them by his knowledge of revealed truth. If they do not comport therewith, he rejects them or at least holds them in abeyance until all the facts are in. His knowledge and faith enable him to distinguish between truth and error. The manner and importance of so doing we learn from Mormon, who said to the saints in his day:

"Take heed, my beloved brethren, that ye do not judge that which is evil to be of God, or that which is good and of God to be of the devil. . . .

"For behold, the Spirit of Christ is given to every man, that he may know good from evil; wherefore, I show unto you the way to judge; for every thing which inviteth to do

11

good, and to persuade to believe in Christ, is sent forth by the power and gift of Christ; wherefore ye may know with a perfect knowledge it is of God.

"But whatsoever thing persuadeth men to do evil, and believe not in Christ, and deny him, and serve not God, then ye may know with a perfect knowledge it is of the devil; for after this manner doth the devil work."

Then he adds this caution: "And now, my brethren, seeing that ye know the light by which ye may judge, which light is the light of Christ, see that ye do not judge wrongfully; for with that same judgment which ye judge ye shall also be judged." (Moroni 7:14-18.)

3. *The possessor of such faith is fortified in his courage to resist temptation and live true to his convictions.*

Consider, for example, Joseph in Egypt. At the very pinnacle of success, when he was prosperous, popular, young, and romantic, he came upon a great temptation—a temptation that, had he yielded to it, would have ruined his life. His master's wife became enamored with him and sought to seduce him. From the record it is clear that Joseph's strength to resist this great temptation and live true to his convictions was derived from his faith, based upon a knowledge of what the Lord had said about adultery. For, said he, "How . . . can I do this great wickedness, and sin against God?" This weighing of Joseph's temptation in terms of sinning against God was possible only because he was informed as to God's commandments. And thus, he being fortified with knowledge and great faith, "It came to pass, as she spake to Joseph day by day, that he hearkened not unto her." (Genesis 39:9-10.)

4. *The possessor of a well-informed faith enjoys peace of mind in the days of trial.*

There is no greater blessing. There comes a time in the life of every soul, be he ever so self-confident and well-adjusted, when without such an inner peace he sinks into the valley of despair.

For the comfort, encouragement, and guidance of the members of his infant Church, the Lord said in August 1830:

"Listen to the voice of Jesus Christ, your Lord, your God, and your Redeemer, whose word is quick and powerful. . . .

"Lift up your hearts and rejoice, and gird up your loins, and take upon you my whole armor, that ye may be able to withstand the evil day, having done all, that ye may be able to stand.

"Stand, therefore, having your loins girt about with truth, having on the breastplate of righteousness, and your feet shod with the preparation of the gospel of peace, which I have sent mine angels to commit unto you;

"Taking the shield of faith wherewith ye shall be able to quench all the fiery darts of the wicked;

"And take the helmet of salvation, and the sword of my Spirit, which I will pour out upon you, and my word which I reveal unto you, and be agreed as touching all things what-soever ye ask of me, and be faithful until I come, and ye shall be caught up, that where I am ye shall be also. Amen." (D&C 27:1, 15-18.)

Great is the power of faith, and great are the rewards for faithfulness!

BE NOT
FAITHLESS

President Gordon B. Hinckley

Every spring the Christian world celebrates Easter in remembrance of the resurrection, when the risen Lord appeared first to Mary Magdalene, and later that day to the ten apostles, Thomas being absent. When the other disciples told Thomas, "We have seen the Lord," he, like so many then and now, said, "Except I shall see in his hands the print of the nails, and put my finger into the print of the nails, and thrust my hand into his side, I will not believe."

Eight days later the apostles were together again, this time Thomas with them. "Then came Jesus, the doors being shut, and stood in the midst, and said, Peace be unto you." Singling out Thomas, He said: "Reach hither thy finger, and behold my hands; and reach hither thy hand, and thrust it into my side: and be not faithless, but believing."

Thomas, astonished and shaken, answered, "My Lord and my God." Then Jesus said to him, "Thomas, because thou hast seen me, thou hast believed: blessed are they that have not seen, and yet have believed." (John 20:25-29.)

Have you not heard others speak as Thomas spoke? "Give us," they say, "the empirical evidence. Prove before our very eyes, and our ears, and our hands, else we will not believe." This is the language of the time in which we live. Thomas the Doubter has become the example of men in all ages who refuse to accept other than that which they can physically prove and explain—as if they could prove love, or faith, or even such physical phenomena as electricity.

To all who may have doubts, I repeat the words given Thomas as he felt the wounded hands of the Lord: "Be not faithless, but believing." Believe in Jesus Christ, the Son of God, the greatest figure of time and eternity. Believe that His matchless life reached back before the world was formed. Believe that He was the Creator of the earth on which we live. Believe that He was Jehovah of the Old Testament, that He was the Messiah of the New Testament, that He died and was resurrected, that He visited these western continents and taught the people here, that He ushered in this final gospel dispensation, and that He lives, the living Son of the living God, our Savior and our Redeemer.

John says of the creation that "all things were made by [God]; and without him was not any thing made that was made." (John 1:3.)

Can any man who has walked beneath the stars at night, can anyone who has seen the touch of spring upon the land doubt the hand of divinity in creation? So observing the beauties of the earth, one is wont to speak as did the Psalmist: "The heavens declare the glory of God; and the firmament sheweth his handywork. Day unto day uttereth speech, and night unto night sheweth knowledge." (Psalm 19:1-2.)

All of beauty in the earth bears the fingerprint of the Master Creator, of those hands which, after they took the form of mortality and then immortality, Thomas insisted on touching before he would believe.

Be not faithless, but believe in Jehovah, He whose finger wrote upon the tablets of stone amid the thunders of Sinai, "Thou shalt have no other gods before me." (Exodus 20:3.) The Decalogue, which is the basis of all good law governing human relations, is the product of His divine genius. As you look upon the vast body of legalisms designed to protect men and society, pause and know that it has its roots in those few brief and timeless declarations given by the all-wise Jehovah to Moses, the leader of Israel.

Believe in Him who was the God of Abraham, Isaac, and Jacob, who was the source of inspiration of all the ancient prophets. They spoke as they were moved upon by the Holy Ghost. They spoke for Him when they rebuked kings, when they chastised the nations, and when as seers they looked forward to the coming of a promised Messiah, declaring by the power of revelation, "Therefore the Lord himself shall give you a sign; Behold, a virgin shall conceive, and bear a son, and shall call his name Immanuel." (Isaiah 7:14.)

15

"And the government shall be upon his shoulder: and his name shall be called Wonderful, Counsellor, The mighty God, The everlasting Father, The Prince of Peace." (Isaiah 9:6.)

Doubt not, but believe that it was He who was born to earth in a manger when there was no room in the inn. Well did an angel ask a prophet who had foreseen these things in vision: "Knowest thou the condescension of God?" (1 Nephi 11:16.) I suppose none of us can fully understand that—how the great Jehovah should come among men, His birth in a manger, among a hated people, in a vassal state. But at His birth there was an angelic chorus that sang of His glory. There were shepherds who worshipped Him. There was a new star in the east. There were wise men who traveled far to bring tribute of gold, frankincense, and myrrh. One can surmise they touched those tiny hands in wonder and awe as they presented their gifts to the newborn king.

Herod the Great, who knew of the prophecies, feared those hands and sought to destroy them; and in the horrible slaughter of the innocents he brought blood upon his own hands and head.

Believe that John the Baptist spoke by the power of revelation when he declared of Jesus, "Behold the Lamb of God, which taketh away the sin of the world." (John 1:29.) And that it was the voice of the Almighty that declared above the waters of Jordan, "This is my beloved Son, in whom I am well pleased." (Matthew 3:17.)

Believe and know that He was a man of miracles. He who had created the world and governed it as the great Jehovah understood the elements of earth and all the functions of life. Beginning at Cana, where He turned the water into wine, He went on to cause the lame to walk, the blind to see, the dead to return to life—He, the Master Physician, who healed the sick by the authority inherent in Him as the Son of God.

He was the comforter of the burdened of His time and of all the generations who have come after who have truly believed in Him. Said He to each of us: "Come unto me, all ye that labour and are heavy laden, and I will give you rest. Take my yoke upon you, and learn of me; for I am meek and lowly in heart: and ye shall find rest unto your souls. For my yoke is easy, and my burden is light." (Matthew 11:28-30.)

I spoke one day to a friend who had escaped from his native land. With the fall of his nation, he had been arrested and interned. His wife and children had been able to get away, but for three years and more he had been a prisoner without means of communication with those he loved. The food had been wretched, the living conditions oppressive, with no prospects for improvement. "What sustained you through all those dark days?" I asked. He responded: "My faith; my faith in the Lord Jesus Christ. I put my burdens on Him, and then they seemed so much lighter."

On one occasion while the Lord was traveling through Samaria, He wearied and thirsted. Pausing at Jacob's well, He rested and requested a drink from the woman who had come to draw water. In the conversation that followed, He declared the saving power of His teaching, saying: "Whosoever drinketh of this water shall thirst again: but whosoever drinketh of the water that I shall give him . . . [it] shall be in him a well of water springing up into everlasting life." (John 4:13-14.)

In that same conversation He declared His identity when the woman at the well spoke of the promised Messiah, "which is called Christ." He, without equivocation, said, "I that speak unto thee am he." (John 4:25-26.)

Doubt not, but believe that He is the Master of life and death. To the sorrowing Martha He declared His eternal power, saying: "I am the resurrection, and the life: he that believeth in me, though he were dead, yet shall he live: and whosoever liveth and believeth in me shall never die." (John 11:25-26.)

Were words so great as these ever spoken for the comfort of those who have lost loved ones? Thomas was present when those words were given and also when Lazarus afterwards was called forth from the tomb. Yet he doubted the Lord's power to bring Himself forth after the terrible death upon the cross, asserting to his fellow apostles that except he feel the wounds in the hands, he would not believe. Small wonder that Jesus rebuked him, saying, "Be not faithless, but believing."

We, like Thomas, are so prone to forget the evidences of His matchless life and power. Those evidences are not found alone in the Bible, the testament of the Old World. There is a testament of the New World that was brought forth by the gift and power of God to the convincing of the Jew and the gentile that Jesus is the Christ. It contains another gospel, beautiful in language and powerful in spirit.

In His earthly ministry Jesus spoke of other sheep of another fold from those He was then teaching and declared that they also should hear His voice, "and there shall be one fold, and one shepherd." (John 10:16.)

At some time following His resurrection, a voice was heard from the heavens among a people who were gathered together in the Land Bountiful somewhere on these western continents. It was the voice of God, and it said unto them: "Behold my Beloved Son, in whom I am well pleased, in whom I have glorified my name—hear ye him.

"And . . . they saw a Man descending out of heaven; and he was clothed in a white robe; and he came down and stood in the midst of them," declaring unto them: "Behold, I am Jesus Christ, whom the prophets testified shall come into the world." He invited them, as He invited Thomas, to feel His hands and side, and they were astonished and cried, "Hosanna! Blessed be the name of the Most High God!" (3 Nephi 11:7-17.)

They doubted not, but believed, as have millions who have read this marvelous witness of the resurrected Lord.

And there is yet another testifier, for as certainly as the voice of God declared the divine Sonship of Jesus at the waters of Jordan, and again on the Mount of Transfiguration, and yet again at the Land Bountiful, even so again that same introduction was made in the opening of this gospel dispensation. It came in a glorious vision in which God the Eternal Father and His Son Jesus Christ appeared and spoke to a young man who had come seeking, and who in the years that followed spoke as a prophet of the risen Lord, even giving his life in testimony of Him who had died upon the cross.

With so many evidences, and with the conviction borne in our hearts by the power of the Holy Ghost, we add in words of soberness and sincerity and love our testimony of the Lord Jesus Christ; wherefore, O man, "be not faithless, but believing" in Him who is the living Son of God, our Savior and our Redeemer.

THE FAITH OF OUR FOUNDING FATHERS

President Ezra Taft Benson

> *Oh beautiful for heroes proved*
> *In liberating strife,*
> *Who more than self their coun-*
> * try loved,*
> *And mercy more than life!* *

The foundation of the United States of America is spiritual. We must never forget this vital truth. This country was founded on a belief in the sovereignty of God, and He, not man, granted man his rights. This was possible because the Founding Fathers of this nation were God-fearing men disposed to deliberately acknowledge the hand of God in the events that brought about the nation's independence.

The Lord raised up the founders of the United States, sanctioned their work, and designated them "wise men." His approbation of their work is recorded in section 101 of the Doctrine and Covenants: "And for this purpose have I established the Constitution of this land, by the hands of wise men whom I raised up unto this very purpose, and redeemed the land by the shedding of blood." (D&C 101:80.)

In 1877, shortly after the dedication of the St. George Temple, the first temple in Utah, the Founding Fathers appeared to Elder Wilford Woodruff, one of the twelve apostles, who was president of the temple. This is his testimony:

"Before I left St. George, the spirits of the [Founding Fathers] gathered around me, wanting to know why we did not redeem them. Said they, 'You have had the use of the Endowment House for a number of years, and yet nothing has ever been done for us. We laid the foundation of the government you now enjoy, and we never apostatized from it,

---

* Katherine Lee Bates, "America, the Beautiful," st. 3.

20

but we remained true to it and were faithful to God.' These were the signers of the Declaration of Independence, and they waited on me for two days and two nights. . . . I straightway went into the baptismal font and called upon Brother McCallister to baptize me for the signers of the Declaration of Independence, and fifty other eminent men, making one hundred in all, including John Wesley, Columbus, and others." (*Journal of Discourses* 19:229.)

At a conference in April 1898, after he became president of the Church, President Woodruff declared:

"Those men who laid the foundation of this American government and signed the Declaration of Independence were the best spirits the God of heaven could find on the face of the earth. They were choice spirits, not wicked men. General Washington and all the men that labored for the purpose were inspired of the Lord. . . .

"Everyone of those men that signed the Declaration of Independence, with General Washington, called upon me, as an Apostle of the Lord Jesus Christ, in the Temple at St. George, two consecutive nights, and demanded at my hands that I should go forth and attend to the ordinances of the House of God for them." (*Conference Report,* April 1898, pp. 89-90.)

Shortly after Spencer W. Kimball became president of the Church, we met together in one of our weekly meetings. We spoke of the sacred records that are in the vaults of the various temples of the Church. As I was soon to fill a conference assignment to St. George, President Kimball asked if I would go into the vault at the temple and check the early records. In so doing, I realized the fulfillment of a dream I had had ever since learning of the visit of the Founding Fathers to this sacred place. I saw with my own eyes the records of the work that was done for the Founding Fathers of this great nation, beginning with George Washington. I was deeply moved on that occasion to realize that these great men returned to this promised land by permission of the Lord and had their ordinance work done for them. If they had not been faithful men, if they had not been God-fearing men, would they have come to the elders of Israel to seek their temple blessings? I think not. *The Lord raised them up, sanctioned their work, and proclaimed them "wise men." Moreover, a president of the Church declared them to be the "best spirits the God of heaven could find on the face of the earth," and testified that they were "choice spirits" and "inspired of the Lord."*

I emphasize this because there have been some efforts recently to belittle their accomplishments and depreciate their integrity—efforts, I might add, that are clearly pointed toward undermining, changing, or destroying the system established by them.

Here was a group of men unparalleled in the history of mankind in their character, foresight, and integrity and with regard to their spiritual awareness that political rights are eternal, inherent, and God-given. "There has not been another such group of men in all the [200] years of our history, no group that even challenged the supremacy of this group." (J. Reuben Clark, Jr., *Conference Report*, April 1957, p. 47.)

The historian Henry Steele Commager queried: "What explains this remarkable outpouring of political leadership, this fertility in the production of statesmen—a fertility unmatched since that day? Was it an historical accident? Was it a peculiar response to the time or the place, or to a combination of the two? Or was it a product of conditions and attitudes that were cultivated and directed to calculated ends, and that can be if not re-created at least paralleled in our time?" ("Leadership in Eighteenth-Century America and Today," *Freedom and Order*, New York: G. Graziller, 1966, pp. 149-50.)

Since these men were foreordained to come to earth to lay the foundation of liberty, this explains why such an aggregation of talent, political wisdom, and faith was concentrated at one time in one place, making this period so extraordinary and exceptional in history.

Who were these "wise men" whom the Lord raised up? They were the more prominent leaders of the American Revolution, which included the period of the Continental

Congress, the Declaration of Independence, and the framing and adoption of the Constitution through the beginning years of the republic.

As indicated by the testimony of Wilford Woodruff and the declaration of the Lord Himself, the Founding Fathers were those who laid the foundation of the American Republic, the fifty-six men who signed the Declaration of Independence and the thirty-nine who signed the Constitution. These were young men, but men of exceptional character, "sober, seasoned, distinguished men of affairs, drawn from various walks of life." (J. Reuben Clark, Jr., *Stand Fast by Our Constitution*, Deseret Book, 1962, p. 135.)

Was their religious faith relevant to what they accomplished? I believe it was most significant because they believed that what they accomplished was not possible without the superintending hand of God, and they believed that morality based on true religion was indispensable to liberty, without which the new republic would fail.

Consider the testimonies of their belief in God, which evidence a conviction and deliberate acknowledgment that God's hand was in the events that brought about our independence.

George Washington: "The success, which has hitherto attended our united efforts, we owe to the gracious interposition of Heaven, and to that interposition let us gratefully ascribe the praise of victory, and the blessings of peace." (To the Executive of New Hampshire, November 3, 1789, *Writings* 30:453.)

Alexander Hamilton: "The Sacred Rights of mankind are not to be rummaged from among old parchments or musty records. They are written . . . by the Hand of Divinity itself." (An Essay, "The Farmer Refuted," 1775.) "For my own part, I sincerely esteem it a system, which without the finger of God, never could have been suggested and agreed upon by such a diversity of interests."

Thomas Jefferson: "The God who gave us life gave us liberty at the same time." (Rights of British America, 1774.)

John Adams: "As I understand the Christian religion, it

23

was, and is, a revelation." (*In God We Trust*, p. 75.)

Benjamin Franklin: "The longer I live the more convincing Proofs I see of this Truth. That God Governs in the Affairs of Men!—And if a Sparrow cannot fall to the Ground without his Notice, is it probable that an Empire can rise without his Aid?—We have been assured, . . . in the Sacred Writings, that 'except the Lord build the House, they labour in vain that build it.' I firmly believe this;—and I also believe that *without* his concurring Aid we shall succeed in this political building no better than Builders of Babel." (Prayer during Constitutional Convention, June 28, 1787.)

James Madison: "It is impossible for the man of pious reflection not to perceive in it a finger of that Almighty hand which has been so frequently and signally extended to our relief in the critical stages of the revolution." (*Federalist Papers*, no. 37.)

Samuel Adams: "Revelation assures us that 'Righteousness exalteth a Nation'—Communities are dealt with in this World by the wise and just Ruler of the Universe. He rewards or punishes them according to their general Character." (Letter to John Scollary, 1776.)

Charles Pickney: "When the great work was done and published, I was . . . struck with amazement. Nothing less than that superintending hand of Providence, that so miraculously carried us through the war, . . . could have brought it about so complete, upon the whole." (P. L. Ford, ed., *Essays on the Constitution*, 1892, p. 412.)

It was not just incidental, nor was it mere political platitude, that the name of God was mentioned in the Declaration of Independence four times and that our inspired national motto became "In God We Trust."

We are not to conclude from the foregoing expressions of religious belief that all of the founders professed a formal faith. Writers and biographers of some of the founders have classified them as deists, which implied that they denied revelation and relied solely on reason. This may have been true in a few exceptional instances, but essentially they were believers in God, immortality, and an eventual judgment day.

They maintained a respect for the Bible and the Judaic-Christian heritage of the nation. None claimed to be an atheist, although some were labeled as such because they rejected certain established tenets of the religious denominations of the day.

Again their testimony to Wilford Woodruff was: "We were faithful to God."

What significance is it to us living today that the founders were God-fearing men of faith?

This nation was founded on certain principles, chief among which was the expressed statement that all men are "endowed by their Creator with certain unalienable rights." This pronouncement recognizes God as the Creator of man and that man's rights are an inherent gift from their Creator.

The founders further recognized that if the new nation were to survive, there must be reliance on the protection of God. The Declaration of Independence concluded with this affirmation: "With a firm reliance on the protection of Divine providence, we mutually pledge to each other our lives, our fortunes, and our sacred honor."

The religious faith of the founders was totally consistent with the Lord's injunction concerning those who would inhabit the land of America:

And now, we can behold the decrees of God concerning this land, that it is a land of promise; and whatsoever nation shall possess it shall serve God, or they shall be swept off when the fulness of his wrath shall come upon them. And the fulness of his wrath cometh upon them when they are ripened in iniquity.

For behold, this is a land which is choice above all other lands; wherefore he that doth possess it shall serve God or shall be swept off; for it is the everlasting decree of God. And it is not until the fulness of iniquity among the children of the land, that they are swept off. . . .

Behold, this is a choice land, and whatsoever nation shall possess it shall be free from bondage, and from captivity, and from all other nations under heaven, *if they will but serve the God of the land, who is Jesus Christ,* who hath been manifested by the things which we have written. (Ether 2:9-10, 12. Italics added.)

In other words, this nation will be preserved so long as we retain the same quality of faith in God that our founders manifested. Personal righteousness is essential to our liberty. The burden of self-government depends on our supporting wise and good representatives, exercising self-restraint, and keeping the commandments of God.

All is not well in our beloved land. Our problems for the most part are directly traceable to the transgression of those sacred laws given to Moses on Mount Sinai over three thousand years ago. These eternal laws were honored by our Founding Fathers. But today worship and service to God have noticeably declined. In the midst of all our prosperity, we may say with Lincoln, "We have forgotten God." Blasphemy, foul stories, and questionable humor characterize films, television programs, and the daily conversations of many Americans. The Sabbath has become a desecrated day of amusement. Idleness, greed, covetousness, cheating, lying, stealing, shoplifting, and immorality are commonplace in our society.

Is this not an evidence that there has been an apostasy from the faith and practice of our founders?

Latter-day Saints stand without excuse. The Lord, through modern revelation as well as statements by the prophets, has given us inspired direction. The Constitution of this land is the only constitution in the world bearing the stamp of approval of the Lord Jesus Christ.

The Lord has said this to us: "I, the Lord God, make you free, therefore ye are free indeed; and the law also maketh you free. Nevertheless, when the wicked rule the people mourn. Wherefore, honest men and wise men should be sought for diligently, and good men and wise men ye should observe to uphold; otherwise whatsoever is less than this cometh of evil." (D&C 98:8-10.)

This nation has a spiritual foundation and a prophetic history. It is, in very deed, the Lord's base of operations in these latter days. From this base the gospel must be carried to all the world, and in order to do this, the nation must be kept strong and sound.

Without faith in God and righteousness, we are no better than any of the other nations that have sunk into oblivion.

Our Founding Fathers, with solemn and reverent expression, voiced their allegiance to the sovereignty of God, knowing that they were accountable to Him in the day of judgment. Are we less accountable today? I think not.

I urge all to keep the commandments and to pray for our nation and its leaders. It is my conviction that God does now look with favor and has looked with favor upon this government, which He established by wise men. It is also my firm conviction that His protective hand is still over the United States of America. I know too that if we will keep the commandments of God—live as He has directed and as He does now direct through His prophets—we will continue to have His protecting hand over us. But we must be true to the great Christian principles that God has revealed. Then, and only then, will we be safe as a nation and as individuals.

God grant that we as members of the Church can stand before God and declare as the founders of this nation did, "We never apostatized. We remained true and were faithful to God."

THE FAITH
OF PROPHETS

Elder Mark E. Petersen

The prophets of God—all of them—walk by faith, just as the rest of us should. Some have seen God, but not all, for it was decreed long ago that the Lord's ministry among the Gentiles would be by the Holy Ghost.

The Savior explained this to the ancient Nephites. He referred to His sermon in Palestine when He told the Jews, "Other sheep I have, which are not of this fold: them also I must bring, and they shall hear my voice; and there shall be one fold, and one shepherd." (John 10:16.)

The Jews supposed that He was speaking of the Gentiles, for He added, "They understood me not that I said they [the other sheep] shall hear my voice; and they understood me not that the Gentiles should not at any time hear my voice— that I should not manifest myself unto them save it were by the Holy Ghost." (3 Nephi 15:23.)

A great principle is announced here: The preaching of the gospel to the Gentiles would be a dispensation of the ministry of the Holy Ghost, and it would not include frequent appearances of the Savior personally.

The Lord did appear to Hebrew prophets at various times, and also to the Nephites. He was seen by Moroni, Mormon, and others—all of them Israelites—and He appeared to congregations of Nephites. Following His resurrection when He first appeared to them, twenty-five hundred people saw the glorious manifestation described in the Book of Mormon. But they were not Gentiles. They were a branch of the house of Israel. They were given both sight and faith, and they labored accordingly.

When the gospel was to be restored in the latter days, it became necessary that the Father and the Son manifest themselves to the prophets to initiate the work. There was an important reason for this. The false notions about God that were being taught among the various congregations of the world must be dispelled. People did not know what God was like. Many creeds taught that He was an indefinable something that filled the whole universe, having no substance, shape, or limitation of size, and was not a person. Others said that the Father and Son in some mysterious way were of one substance or body, yet separate, in a contradiction of terms that was admittedly unexplainable. At least one creed taught that God was sheer intelligence, distributed everywhere in the universe, and that when we die, our intelligence merges with the over-all intelligence, and that that constitutes immortality for us.

To restore the gospel and provide a basis for a solid faith, it was necessary that a true knowledge of God be restored. This was accomplished in the first vision of the Prophet Joseph Smith, wherein he saw both the Father and the Son as separate, glorified persons in whose image human beings were made.

This glorious event became the basis for the restoration of the gospel. It provided the means whereby people could believe in God as a person, as our eternal Father in heaven, and in the Savior, also as a divine but individual being, separate from the Father but in the form of man. Jesus lived as a man on earth, and He was resurrected also as a man without losing His form or identity.

Joseph Smith and Oliver Cowdery saw the Savior as a divine individual in the Kirtland Temple. (See D&C 110.) Angels also came to restore their powers and blessings.

Joseph Smith and Sidney Rigdon had the glorious vision described in section 76 of the Doctrine and Covenants. The Savior also appeared to some at the dedication of the Kirtland Temple. A few other appearances of the Savior to our modern prophets are also recorded. For the most part, however, the taking of the gospel to the Gentile nations is a ministry of the Holy Ghost and does not require the personal appearance and visitations of the Lord Jesus Christ.

There is no record that the Savior appeared to the Gentile nations visited by Paul, and for the same reason. The

Gentiles were to receive the gospel through the Holy Ghost. Is He not one of the Godhead? Does He not bear witness of Christ and give to modern people, Israelites or Gentiles, a testimony of the truth?

The Lord Himself said that the Holy Ghost, the Comforter, bears testimony of Him. (See John 15:26.) Paul, writing to the Corinthians, said: "Wherefore I give you to understand, that no man speaking by the Spirit of God calleth Jesus accursed: and that no man can say that Jesus is the Lord, but by the Holy Ghost." (1 Corinthians 12:3.) And wasn't Paul the apostle to the Gentiles?

In our day, some have seen the Savior, but the major part of today's ministry is through the Holy Ghost. How do revelations come for work among the Gentiles?

When Paul and Barnabas were chosen to go forth among the Gentiles, how did their call come? Through the Holy Ghost! Note these words:

"Now there were in the church that was at Antioch certain prophets and teachers; as Barnabas, and Simeon that was called Niger, and Lucius of Cyrene, and Manaen, which had been brought up with Herod the tetrarch, and Saul. As they ministered to the Lord, and fasted, the Holy Ghost said, Separate me Barnabas and Saul for the work whereunto I have called them.

"And when they had fasted and prayed, and laid their hands on them, they sent them away. So they, being sent forth by the Holy Ghost, departed unto Seleucia; and from thence they sailed to Cyprus." (Acts 13:1-3.)

The Holy Ghost, of course, ministered to the Israelite prophets. Alma says that he also received manifestations by the Holy Ghost. (Alma 5:46.) The Holy Ghost bore witness to the Nephites of both the Father and the Son. (2 Nephi 31:18; 3 Nephi 11:36.) He therefore was not in any manner limited to the Gentile ministry, but the Gentile ministry in large measure was limited to the Holy Ghost.

In our day what did the Lord say to the Prophet Joseph Smith? Note these words: "I speak unto you with my voice, even the voice of my Spirit, that I may show unto you my will concerning your brethren in the land of Zion, many of whom are truly humble and are seeking diligently to learn wisdom and to find truth." (D&C 97:1.)

The elders of that day were to work as they were guided by the Spirit: "But notwithstanding those things which are written, it always has been given to the elders of my church from the beginning, and ever shall be, to conduct all meetings as they are directed and guided by the Holy Spirit." (D&C 46:2.)

The Holy Ghost was a revelator to our early leaders. He gave them utterance (D&C 14:8), and manifested to them all that was expedient for them to know (D&C 18:18). The Twelve were told to speak by the power of the Holy Ghost (D&C 18:32). The prophets of our day were to speak as they were inspired by the Holy Ghost, which testifies of Christ (D&C 20:26-27). The meetings of our early brethren were to be conducted under the inspiration of the Holy Ghost (D&C 20:45), and the officers of the Church were to be ordained under His guidance (D&C 20:60).

One of the interesting scriptures regarding the brethren laboring under the power of the Holy Ghost is this: "And this is the ensample unto them, that they shall speak as they are moved upon by the Holy Ghost. And whatsoever they shall speak when moved upon by the Holy Ghost shall be scripture, shall be the will of the Lord, shall be the mind of the Lord, shall be the word of the Lord, shall be the voice of the Lord, and the power of God unto salvation." (D&C 68:3-4.)

The Lord made it clear that Joseph was inspired by the Holy Ghost in laying the foundation of this Church. (D&C 21:2.)

Since the Church today carries the gospel abroad to the Gentiles, the work conforms to the dispensation of the Holy Ghost. It is not necessary for the Savior to make numerous and repeated appearances when the Holy Ghost is directing this ministry as a member of the Godhead.

The Prophet Joseph Smith taught:

When the Twelve or any other witnesses stand before the congregations of the earth, and they preach in the power and demonstration of the

Spirit of God, and the people are astonished and confounded at the doctrine, and say, "That man has preached a powerful discourse, a great sermon, then let that man or those men take care that they do not ascribe the glory unto themselves, but be careful that they are humble, and ascribe the praise and glory to God and the Lamb; for it is by the power of the Holy Priesthood and the Holy Ghost that they have power thus to speak. What art thou, O man, but dust? And from whom receivest thou thy power and blessings, but from God?

Then, O ye Twelve! notice this *Key*, and be wise for Christ's sake, and your own soul's sake. Ye are not sent out to be taught, but to teach. Let every word be seasoned with grace. Be vigilant; be sober. It is a day of warning, and not of many words. Act honestly before God and man. Beware of Gentile sophistry; such as bowing and scraping unto men in whom you have no confidence. Be honest, open, and frank in all your intercourse with mankind.

O ye Twelve! and all Saints! profit by this important *Key*—that in all your trials, troubles, temptations, afflictions, bonds, imprisonments and death, see to it, that you do not betray heaven; that you do not betray Jesus Christ; that you do not betray the brethren; that you do not betray the revelations of God, whether in the Bible, Book of Mormon, or Doctrine and Covenants, or any other that ever was or ever will be given and revealed unto man in this world or that which is to come. Yea, in all your kicking and flounderings, see to it that you do not this thing, lest innocent blood be found upon your skirts, and you go down to hell. All other sins are not to be compared to sinning against the Holy Ghost, and proving a traitor to the brethren.

I will give you one of the *Keys* of the mysteries of the Kingdom. It is an eternal principle, that has existed with God from all eternity: That man who rises up to condemn others, finding fault with the Church, saying that they are out of the way, while he himself is righteous, then know assuredly, that that man is in the high road to apostasy; and if he does not repent, will apostatize, as God lives. The principle is as correct as the one that Jesus put forth in saying that he who seeketh a sign is an adulterous person; and that principle is eternal, undeviating, and firm as the pillars of heaven; for whenever you see a man seeking after a sign, you may set it down that he is an adulterous man. (*History of the Church* 3:384-85.)

The Prophet made it clear that the guidance of the Holy Ghost was part of that ministry, since the Holy Ghost is a revelator. It is by that power that the Church is guided to the Gentiles in this dispensation.

Faith in the lives of the prophets? It is the basis and foundation of their testimonies. By this faith they do their work, carrying on their ministry to all the world.

The apostle Paul taught that in the Church are apostles, prophets, evangelists, pastors, and teachers, "for the perfecting of the saints, for the work of the ministry, for the edifying of the body of Christ: till we all come in the unity of the faith, and of the knowledge of the Son of God, unto a perfect man, unto the measure of the stature of the fulness of Christ: that we henceforth be no more children, tossed to and fro, and carried about with every wind of doctrine, by the sleight of men, and cunning craftiness, whereby they lie in wait to deceive." (Ephesians 4:12-14.)

And how was all of this to be done? By the inspiration and direction of the Holy Ghost!

The prophets teach faith—through the power of the Holy Ghost.

They teach repentance by the same power.

They teach perfection of the Saints by the same power.

They teach unity among the Saints by the same power.

They help us to obtain "the knowledge of the Son of God, unto a perfect man, unto the measure of the stature of the fulness of Christ."

This is all done by the power of the Holy Ghost. That is the way our prophets teach; that is the way they live; that is the way they direct the work of the Lord in these last days. This gives us encouragement to obtain faith like theirs, that the gospel will indeed be as real to us as it is to them.

Yes, the prophets walk by faith!

FAITH:
THE FIRST STEP

Elder Howard W. Hunter

Christians throughout the world each year celebrate the event considered by them to be the greatest happening in recorded history—the occasion when the Lord and Master arose from the tomb to live again, after having been put to death on the cross. This event has been celebrated each spring for more than nineteen hundred years. We are reminded, when the day comes, that the cold, dark winter has drawn to a close, and all nature is ready to come to life.

After the snows have melted away, trees and shrubs put forth new shoots, buds commence to burst, and all the earth becomes a symphony of warmth and color, assuring us of new life. The change of nature from the chill of winter to the beauty of spring recalls the change from the gloom and despair of Gethsemane to the glorious event of the resurrection. The stone was rolled away and the announcement made: "He is not here, but is risen." (Luke 24:6.)

The reality of the event of the resurrection has profound meaning to every person who has the courage to believe. Is it true? Is Jesus Christ a reality? Did He actually come to earth, proclaim His gospel, and give His life for mankind? Is it true that He was resurrected from the tomb to make it possible for you and me to live again after death and have life everlasting? What evidence is there of these things? How do we gain a knowledge of the truth of them if we do not know?

I believe these things with all my heart. I know they are true. I know that God lives and is literally our Heavenly Father; that Jesus Christ is His Son, the Redeemer of the world; and that through His atoning sacrifice, every man who lives upon the earth, or who has lived or will live upon the earth, will be resurrected after death to live again. My belief in this regard has come in the same way as it has to

34

others who believe. All persons could have this understanding by following this simple scriptural admonition:

"Ask, and it shall be given you; seek, and ye shall find; knock, and it shall be opened unto you; For every one that asketh receiveth; and he that seeketh findeth; and to him that knocketh it shall be opened." (Matthew 7:7-8.)

In his letter to Israel, James cast the admonition in words with similar meaning: "If any of you lack wisdom, let him ask of God, that giveth to all men liberally, and upbraideth not; and it shall be given him. But let him ask in faith, nothing wavering. For he that wavereth is like a wave of the sea driven with the wind and tossed." (James 1:5-6.)

There are some who believe and others who doubt, but questions can be resolved and knowledge gained if we will follow these simple instructions from the scriptures. Of course, those who lack the desire to know and are "driven by the wind and tossed" will never understand the things pertaining to God and his divine plan. A prophet has made this meaningful statement:

"The things of God are of deep import; and time, and experience, and careful and ponderous and solemn thoughts can only find them out. Thy mind, O man! if thou wilt lead a soul unto salvation, must stretch as high as the utmost heavens, and search into and contemplate the darkest abyss, and the broad expanse of eternity—thou must commune with God." (*History of the Church* 3:295.)

The gospel, as brought to the earth by the Savior, is the good news of salvation; therefore, the plan of salvation *is* the gospel of Jesus Christ. He said, "Remember the things that I have told you. Behold I have given unto you my gospel, and this is the gospel which I have given unto you—that I came into the world to do the will of my Father, because my Father sent me. And my Father sent me that I might be lifted up upon the cross; and after that I had been lifted up upon the cross, that I might draw all men unto me, that as I have been lifted up by men even so should men be lifted up by the Father, to stand before me, to be judged of their works, whether they be good or whether they be evil." (3 Nephi 27:12-14.)

As we study the scriptures carefully, the understanding comes to us that the basic elements or principles of the gospel taught by the Master consist of the following steps:

1. We must develop within ourselves faith in Jesus Christ, that He is the Son of God and the Savior of the world.

2. We must repent of wrongdoings and be willing to follow His teachings.

3. We must be baptized according to instruction for a remission of past sins.

4. We must receive the Holy Ghost by the laying on of hands.

5. We must continue in righteous living to the end of mortal life.

The first step is faith, not just faith in general, but a specific faith—faith in the Lord Jesus Christ. To know whether or not Jesus Christ is a reality, or if it is true that He is the Son of God and came to earth to proclaim His gospel, give His life, and accomplish the resurrection that all men may live again, there must arise within one's soul a genuine desire to gain a knowledge of the truth. When such a desire becomes strong enough, we are persuaded to examine the evidence.

There is no tangible, concrete evidence of the existence of God or the divinity of the Master in the legal sense, but not all inquiry for truth results in proof by real or demonstrative evidence. It is fallacious to argue that because there is no demonstrative evidence of the existence of God, He does not in fact exist. In the absence of evidence often thought necessary by the scientific world for positive proof, our search may take us into the realm of circumstantial evidence. We could spend hours describing the wonders of the universe, of the earth, of nature, and of the human body, the exactness of the laws of physics, and a thousand things, all of which dictate to the conscience of a truth seeker that there is a Creator and One who rules over the universe.

What would be the situation if the existence of God could be proven by demonstrative evidence? What would happen to the element of faith as the first step or principle of the gospel? One of the burdens of the teachings of the Master was to emphasize the importance of faith. Faith is the element that builds the bridge in the absence of concrete evidence. This is exactly what the writer of the epistle to the Hebrews was talking about when he referred to faith as "the substance of things hoped for, the evidence of things not seen." (Hebrews 11:1.) In other words, faith is the assurance of the existence of a truth even though it is not evident or cannot be proved by positive evidence.

Suppose that all things could be proven by demonstrative evidence. What then would become of the element of faith? There would be no need for faith and it would be eliminated, giving rise then to this query: If faith is the first step or principle of the gospel and is eliminated, what happens to the gospel plan? The very foundation will crumble. I submit that there is a divine reason why all things cannot be proven by concrete evidence.

Those who doubt are prone to ask for proof or a sign that they might believe. The prophet Alma spoke to his people on this very subject and said to them, "Yea, there are many who do say: If thou wilt show unto us a sign from heaven, then we shall know of a surety; then we shall believe. Now I ask, is this faith? Nay; for if a man knoweth a thing he hath no cause to believe, for he knoweth it." (Alma 32:17-18.)

Alma then talked to his people about the principle of faith and likened it unto a tree seed that, after being planted, needed care and cultivation. The desire for fruit caused the seed to be planted, and the planter had faith that it would sprout and grow. Alma continues to describe this seed of faith:

"As the tree beginneth to grow, ye will say: Let us nourish it with great care, that it may get root, that it may grow up, and bring forth fruit unto us. And now behold, if ye nourish it with much care it will get root, and grow up, and bring forth fruit.

"But if ye neglect the tree, and take no thought for its nourishment, behold it will not get any root; and when the heat of the sun cometh and scorcheth it, because it hath no root it withers away, and ye pluck it up and cast it out.

"Now, this is not because the seed was not good, neither is it because the fruit thereof would not be desirable; but it is because your ground is barren, and ye will not nourish the tree, therefore ye cannot have the fruit thereof.

"And thus, if ye will not nourish the word, looking forward with an eye of faith to the fruit thereof, ye can never pluck of the fruit of the tree of life." (Alma 32:37-40.)

Thus faith becomes the first step in any action and must be the first step in understanding the gospel. Faith in the Lord Jesus Christ brings us to a knowledge of the reality of His atoning sacrifice. We have need to be taught and to understand this first principle.

In the closing two verses of Matthew is given the account of the final appearance of the Master to the eleven disciples on the mountain in Galilee. His parting words emphasize the importance of His teachings and confer the great commission on others to teach all persons: "Go ye therefore, and teach all nations, baptizing them in the name of the Father, and of the Son, and of the Holy Ghost: teaching them to observe all things whatsoever I have commanded you: and, lo, I am with you alway, even unto the end of the world." (Matthew 28:19-20.)

The emphasis is on the words *teach* and *baptize*. Following this scriptural admonition, missionaries of the Church, both young and old, are in the world teaching to all who will hear the principle of faith in the Lord Jesus Christ and the other principles of the gospel. This is according to the pattern established by the Master Himself, as recorded by Mark: "And he called unto him the twelve, and began to send them forth by two and two." (Mark 6:7.) They went forth and bore witness of his divinity in those days, and devoted ambassadors of today bear the same witness as they go into the world "two and two."

The nations of the world will be blessed by the message of

the gospel these missionaries carry, and every person who has an honest desire for the truth, if he will give heed to the message, will learn to know the true and living God and that Jesus is the Christ, the Redeemer of all mankind by His atoning sacrifice. May the faith of each of us be strengthened by conscientious effort.

WHAT IS FAITH?

Elder Boyd K. Packer

During World War II the city of Osaka, Japan, was almost obliterated. Her buildings were rubble, and her streets were littered with blocks, debris, and bomb craters. The subway had been protected, and soon after the occupation, it became the only means of transportation for the city.

One beautiful day in late fall, several servicemen and I came up the steps from the subway. As far as we could see lay the desolation of war. What had been a broad thoroughfare lined with sycamore trees was now a scene of hopeless destruction. Although most of the trees had been blasted completely away, some few of them still stood with shattered limbs and trunks. One or two of them had gathered the courage to send out a few new shoots and had produced a meager crop of foliage.

A gentle breeze was scattering the yellow leaves among the debris. A tiny Japanese girl in a tattered kimono was busily climbing over the rubble, gathering the sycamore leaves into a bouquet. The little sprite of a child seemed unimpressed with the devastation and hopeless futility that surrounded her and was scrambling over the rubble to add new leaves to her collection. She had found the one beautiful element in her world—perhaps it would be more proper to say that *she* was the one beautiful element in the scene.

I have not forgotten that little girl. Somehow, to think of her increases my faith. Embodied in the child was the answer to futility; in her there was hope.

Children have a frankness and honesty that is disarming. They possess a simple, implicit faith that is shared by few adults. The Lord instructed his disciples by calling "a little child unto him, and set him in the midst of them, and said, Verily I say unto you, Except ye be converted, and become as little children, ye shall not enter into the kingdom of heaven." (Matthew 18:2-3.)

In children there is little pride and little vanity. They eagerly and trustingly respond.

It is little wonder that the Lord chose a mere boy to act as his spokesman in restoring the kingdom of God to the earth. Some have been incredulous over the fact—and it is a fact—that God the Father and His Son Jesus Christ did reveal themselves to Joseph Smith when he was but in his fifteenth year. More remarkable perhaps than the vision itself was the naive, implicit faith with which the boy had sought answer to his prayers in a secluded grove.

Faith and humility go hand in hand. The person who can acknowledge his dependence upon God and accept a child-parent relationship with Him has prepared a growing place for faith.

The Book of Mormon gives an account of a man who had tremendous faith. The brother of Jared went up on the mountain with sixteen small stones. He had in mind having the Lord touch them so that there might be light in their vessels as his people traveled. His petition was granted, and as the Lord touched the stones, the brother of Jared saw His finger. He fell down before Him, saying that he knew not that He had flesh and blood. The Lord said unto him: "Because of thy faith thou hast seen that I shall take upon me flesh and blood; and never has man come before me with such exceeding faith as thou hast, for were it not so ye could not have seen my finger. Sawest thou more than this?" The answer was monumentally courageous: "Nay; Lord, show thyself unto me."

In the Lord's answer, the choice of a simple word, the word *shall,* is a marvelous commentary on faith. Now there was a test of faith involved, as the Lord asked: "Believest thou the words which I *shall* speak?" Interesting, isn't it, that he was not asked, "Believest thou the words that I *have* spoken?" It didn't relate to the past. It related to the future. The brother of Jared was asked to commit himself on something that had not yet happened. He was to confirm his belief in that which the Lord had not yet spoken. There are few individuals, indeed, who would command such faith from any of us. To few people would we commit ourselves to believe what they were going to say. It takes faith to be willing to commit oneself that way.

The Lord said, by way of testing the brother of Jared, "Believest thou the words which I *shall* speak?" The brother of Jared confirmed his great faith by answering, "Yea, Lord, I know that thou speakest the truth, for thou art a God of truth, and canst not lie." When the Lord saw that Jared would believe anything He said, He showed Himself to him. The brother of Jared had actually seen; now he had knowledge. The record confirms:

"And because of the knowledge of this man he could not be kept from beholding within the veil; and he saw the finger of Jesus, which, when he saw, he fell with fear; for he knew that it was the finger of the Lord; and he had faith no longer, for he knew, nothing doubting." (Ether 3:1-19.)

Faith, to be faith, must center around something that is not known. Faith, to be faith, must go beyond that for which there is confirming evidence. Faith, to be faith, must go into the unknown. Faith, to be faith, must walk to the edge of the light, and then a few steps into the darkness. If everything has to be known, if everything has to be explained, if everything has to be certified, then there is no need for faith. Indeed, there is no room for it.

The prophet Alma said: "Yea, there are many who do say: If thou wilt show unto us a sign from heaven, then we shall know of a surety; then we shall believe. Now I ask, is that faith? Behold, I say unto you, Nay; for if a man knoweth a thing he hath no cause to believe, for he knoweth it. . . . And now as I said concerning faith—faith is not to have a perfect knowledge of things; therefore if ye have faith ye hope for things which are not seen, which are true." (Alma 32:17-18, 21.)

There are two kinds of faith. One of them functions ordinarily in the life of every soul. It is the kind of faith born by experience; it gives us certainty that a new day will dawn, that spring will come, that growth will take place. It is the kind of faith that relates us with confidence to that which is scheduled to happen. This kind of faith was exemplified by the little Japanese girl.

There is another kind of faith, rare indeed. This is the kind of faith that *causes* things to happen. It is the kind of faith that is worthy and prepared and unyielding, and it calls forth things that otherwise would not be. It is the kind of faith that moves people. It is the kind of faith that sometimes moves things. Few men possess it. It comes by gradual growth. It is a marvelous, even a transcendent, power, a power as real and as invisible as electricity. Directed and channeled, it has great effect.

But faith must be faith. One man tried "experimenting" with faith. He had spoken of his certainty that an event would transpire, and his desires were not brought to pass; the event he so much yearned for did not happen. Afterward, his bitter comment was, "Well, you see, it didn't happen. I didn't think it would."

In a world filled with skepticism and doubt, the expression "seeing is believing" promotes the attitude, "You show me, and I will believe." We want all of the proof and all of the evidence first. It seems hard to take things on faith.

When will we learn that in spiritual things it works the other way about—that believing is seeing? Spiritual belief precedes spiritual knowledge. When we believe in things that are not seen but are nevertheless true, then we have faith.

The Prophet Joseph Smith declared: "Never get discouraged. . . . If I was sunk in the lowest pit of Nova Scotia and all the Rocky Mountains piled on top of me, I . . . hang on, exercise faith and keep up good courage and I should come out on the top." (George A. Smith, *Memoirs of George A. Smith*, pp. 81-82.)

Faith can increase. It will move forward as a light before

us. Sometimes the fogs and mists of doubt are so thick and enshroud us so fully that only the most penetrating and persistent faith will send a beam beyond it.

As we exercise faith we can do as did Nephi, who said: "And I was led by the Spirit, not knowing beforehand the things which I should do." (1 Nephi 4:6.)

FAITH IN
ONESELF

Elder Marvin J. Ashton

In The Church of Jesus Christ of Latter-day Saints, the individual, the human soul, is of utmost importance. We are the sons and daughters of God. He loves us. He wants us to have joy and happiness and to be exalted and dwell with Him. He has said, "This is my work and my glory—to bring to pass the immortality and eternal life of man" (Moses 1:39) and "Remember the worth of souls is great in the sight of God" (D&C 18:10).

Each of us and our lives are important to God. We need to be constantly aware of the fact that we are children of God. He knows us. He hears us. He loves us. His church, His truths, and His eternal dwelling places are for those who love Him, keep His commandments, and continue in His word. We need to constantly remember that faith in God is reflected in faith in oneself, and faith in oneself is manifest by one's actions.

Proper self-image will help us keep our habits, lives, and souls directed in happy paths. How proud we should be in the knowledge that we have Godlike attributes. It was Abraham Lincoln who said, "It is difficult to make a man miserable while he feels he is worthy of himself and claims kindred to the great God who made him."

One of life's eternal pursuits is learning to know oneself. Dr. Thomas Harris shares this worthy thought with us: "Most people never fulfill their human promise and potential because they remain perpetually helpless children overwhelmed by a sense of inferiority. The feeling of being okay does not imply that the person has risen above all his faults and emotional problems. It merely implies that he refuses to be paralyzed by them. He is determined to accept himself as he is but also to assume more and more control of his life."

Getting better acquainted with oneself and realizing God has given to every person gifts and talents is a worthy challenge, "for there are many gifts, and to every man is given a gift by the Spirit of God. To some is given one, and to some is given another, that all may be profited thereby." (D&C 46:11-12.)

How important are you in your own eyes? Do you treat yourself shabbily? Do you forget you are a temple of God? Or do you treat yourself as being a person of great worth? Do you look upon yourself as though you really are a son or daughter of God? Do you have personal respect and honor for yourself? Do you have faith in yourself?

In all of these questions we need to realize that with God's help, we can accomplish all things; our potential is unlimited. What a blessing it is to us individually to know that if we walk in His paths, we can merit security. God's joy is great when we repent and come unto Him. All that God has is available to His worthy children regardless of how long they have been away or lost.

We are all different. God in His wisdom has so created us. Only we can determine what we will do with what happens to us. What we do with what happens to us is more important than what happens to us. Certainly with God's help we can do what is right. The truth "for as he thinketh in his heart, so is he" (Proverbs 23:7) is as applicable today as any time in history.

Shakespeare had a glimpse of the importance of becoming well acquainted with oneself when he wrote the following lines in the play *Hamlet*:

> *This above all: to thine own self be true,*
> *And it must follow, as the night the day,*
> *Thou canst not then be false to any man.*

Being true to ourselves can mean knowing where we are, where we are going and why, and assisting our associates in traveling the right paths with us.

Proper self-management is a great virtue that can lead to personal pride. Personal pride is a great motivator. It is a virtue to understand who we are and to conduct ourselves accordingly. To be created in God's image is a tremendous blessing with accompanying choice responsibilities. He said, "Know ye not that ye are the temple of God, and that the Spirit of God dwelleth in you? If any man defile the temple of God, him shall God destroy; for the temple of God is holy, which temple ye are." (1 Corinthians 3:16-17.)

Appropriate personal pride prohibits shabby performance. Proper self-image is a basic ingredient of pride in oneself. It is necessary if individual discipline is to be purposeful and effective.

Generally the cover or jacket of a book is designed to sell what is inside. We will not have to die to be judged by the cover of the book of life. To those who say, "It's what you really are inside that counts, not the length of the hair or beard," I would say, "If this is true, and I agree it is, why run the risk of looking like something you're not?"

One winter when the Salt Lake area was experiencing one of its worst snowstorms, a handsome young serviceman and his beautiful bride-to-be encountered extreme difficulty in getting to the Salt Lake Temple for their marriage appointment. She was in one location in the valley, and he was to come from another nearby town. Heavy snows and winds had closed the highways during the night and early morning hours. After many hours of anxious waiting, some of us were able to help them get to the temple to be married before the day was over. How grateful they, their families, and their friends were for assistance and concern in their keeping this most important appointment.

The young bridegroom expressed his deep gratitude with these words: "Thank you very much for all you did to make our wedding possible. I don't understand why you went to all this trouble to help me. Really, I'm nobody." I am sure he meant his comment to be a most sincere compliment, but I responded firmly, but I hope kindly, "Bill, I have never helped a 'nobody' in my life. In the kingdom of our Heavenly Father, nobody is a 'nobody.'"

This tendency to wrongfully identify ourselves was again brought to my attention during an interview with a troubled wife. Her marriage was in great difficulty. She had tried earnestly to correct the communication blocks with her husband but with little success. She was grateful for the time her bishop spent in counseling. Her stake president was also most patient and understanding in his willingness to try to help. Her many contacts with properly channeled priesthood direction left her not only grateful but also somewhat amazed. Her concluding observation was, "I just don't understand all of you people giving so much time and showing so much concern. After all, I'm really nobody."

I am certain our Heavenly Father is displeased when we refer to ourselves as "nobody." How fair are we when we classify ourselves as a "nobody"? How fair are we to our families? How fair are we to God? We do ourselves a great injustice when we allow ourselves, through tragedy, misfortune, challenge, discouragement, or whatever the earthly situation, to so identify ourselves.

No matter how or where we find ourselves, we cannot with any justification label ourselves "nobody." As children of God, we are somebody. He will build us, mold us, and magnify us if we will but hold our heads up, our arms out, and walk with Him. What a great blessing to be created in His image and know of our true potential in and through Him! What a great blessing to know that in His strength we can do all things!

God help us to realize that one of our greatest responsibilities and privileges is to lift a self-labeled "nobody" to a "somebody" who is wanted, needed, and desirable. Our first obligation in this area of stewardship is to begin with self. "I am nobody" is a destructive philosophy. It is a tool of the deceiver.

It is heartbreaking when youth in difficulty look up and respond to offered guidance with, "What does it matter? I'm nobody." It is just as disturbing when a student on campus responds with, "I am no one special on campus. I'm just one of the thousands. I'm really nobody."

We are living in days when it is easy to be discontented, tired, fatigued, bored, and vexed in and with life. Discouragement and weariness set in when we allow ourselves the dangerous luxury of self-pity. Such thoughts as these come to us when we allow ourselves to become discouraged and weary: "No one appreciates me." "Even my own children won't listen to me." "I don't have to get involved with someone else." "I'm really not accomplishing anything."

Proper attitude in this crisis-dominated world is a priceless possession. Never before has it been more important for all of us to move forward with conviction. We may be behind, but we are not losing if we are moving in the right direction. God will not score our performance until the end of the journey. He who made us expects us to be victorious. He stands by anxious to answer our call for help.

Sad but true, many today are behind in their contacts with God and are encouraging destructive attitudes toward self and fellowmen. We need to lead with good cheer, optimism, and courage if we are to move onward and upward.

We came into this life for experience, and that's all we can take out of it. Thank God we have the right to decide personally and individually what we shall do. The future belongs to those who know what to do with it. We must look forward to the unknown with optimism and confidence; look to tomorrow with happy expectancy, realizing that with God's help we can do all things. We need to constantly build faith in ourselves and those about us. We need to personally make dark days brighter. Isn't it a joy, a lift, a light, to see someone with heavy challenges and burdens moving forward to victory in the only contest that really matters!

Faith makes it possible for us to know that even in temporary failure or setback, there is always a next time, ever a tomorrow. One of the greatest tragedies of our times is that children of God are living and performing below their capabilities. What a thrill it is to see people achieving, conquering, overcoming through proper daily action, self-discipline, and commitment. Progression and achievement belong to those who have learned to use the opportunity of now. Our strides of today will determine our location tomorrow.

Our obligation is to avoid self-pity, self-judgment, and self-indulgence. If we properly understand our relationship to God and His to us, we will not have moments, days, or lives spent in wondering, "What have I done to deserve this?" "What does God have against me?" or "Why wasn't I born with the talents my friends have?"

Following a recent discussion on the subject of adversity, a young man who was greatly concerned about the burdens being carried by his wonderful mother asked, "If God is omnipotent and knows all, why does He put my mother through the agony of continual sufferings when He already knows what the outcome will be?" My response to him was, "Your mother's trials are not tests so the Lord can measure her. They are tests and trials so that your mother can measure herself. It is most important that she know her strengths in adversity and grow from the experiences."

It is not our role to be self-condemning. I like to think that the admonition of the Savior, "Judge not, that ye be not judged," has direct reference to us and our relationship with ourselves. We should not judge ourselves.

Let me share with you an example of the results of daily determination and performance.

In 1960 the Olympics were held in Melbourne, Australia. In the spotlight on the winner's platform one day there stood a beautiful, tall, blonde American girl. She was being presented a gold medal, symbolic of first place in worldwide competition. Tears ran down her cheeks as she accepted the recognition. Many thought she was touched by the victory ceremony; the thing they did not know was the story of her determination, self-discipline, and daily action.

At the age of five she had polio. When the disease left her body, she couldn't use her arms or legs. Her parents took her every day to a swimming pool, where they hoped the water would help hold her arms up as she tried to use them again. When she could lift her arms out of the water with her own power, she cried with joy. Then her goal was to swim the width of the pool, then the length, then several lengths. Kelly Mann kept on trying, swimming, enduring day after day after day until she won the gold medal for the butterfly stroke—one of the most difficult of all strokes in swimming—at the Olympics in Melbourne.

What shall we do then? Let us resolve to so live that the Lord can say to us, as He did to the Prophet Joseph Smith in some of his darkest, most trying hours, "My son, peace be unto thy soul; thine adversity and thine afflictions shall be but a small moment; and then, if thou endure it well, God shall exalt thee on high; thou shalt triumph over all thy foes." (D&C 121:7-8.)

We should teach ourselves patience—patience to believe in ourselves, patience to motivate ourselves, patience to believe that God and we can do it. When necessary, we should lean on the truth that we are children of God. God and we, with patience on our part, can do it. We do not have to worry about the patience of God, because He is the personification of patience, no matter where we have been, what we have done, or what we have allowed ourselves to think of ourselves.

From Harry Emerson Fosdick we read: "The most extraordinary thing about the oyster is this: Irritations get into his shell. He does not like them. But when he cannot get rid of them, he uses the irritation to do the loveliest thing an oyster ever has a chance to do. If there are irritations in our lives today, there is only one prescription: make a pearl. It may have to be a pearl of patience, but anyhow, make a pearl. And it takes faith and love to do it."

Two of Satan's greatest tools are impatience and discouragement. Drugs, moral misconduct, and violent protest are merely evidences of internal impatience on our part.

A notion commonly shared by many is that the best of life is just ahead, over the next hill, a few years away—retirement, tomorrow, next month, when I turn sixteen, or next summer. We become actively engaged in the pastime of conditioning ourselves to believe that happiness and achievement are always somewhere in the future. There is an attitude of tolerating today, even looking past today in anticipation of a better tomorrow. To people so inclined, the better future may never come. The pleasant future belongs to those who properly use today. We need to find the abundant life as we go along. How can we be happy tomorrow if our nows are filled with self-inflicted unhappiness and unwise delays?

Generally speaking, those inclined to count their blessings have more to count because they help make more possible as they learn gratitude. A constant waiting for a brighter future may cause us to lose the beautiful today. Some spend so much time getting ready to live for an unknown future that they discover there is suddenly no time left to live. Often in our anxiousness for the joys of the future we run away from the very things we are wanting and needing today. An appropriate examination of the passing moment will prove that it leads to eternity. We need to constantly remind ourselves that eternity is in process now.

When the wise counsel that "men should be anxiously engaged in a good cause, and do many things of their own free will, and bring to pass much righteousness" (D&C 58:27) was given, the time structure referred only to now, today, and without delay. How unwise are those who want to delay repentance until tomorrow. With each passing day, the process becomes more difficult to pursue. Most of our hurts and misunderstandings could be cleared away if we treated them today instead of waiting for them to go away tomorrow.

To live more fully each hour and to glean the most from each day is wisdom. How unwise we are to waste our todays, when they determine the significance of our tomorrows. We should wisely live a day at a time, because that is all we have.

Fears in our lives can be conquered if we will but have faith and move forward with purpose. The constant nursing of personal hurts is a crutch for those who would move with hesitation, if at all. Yielding to the pains of tragedy and grief deters self-development and takes away the opportunity for triumph over trying obstacles. Being fettered with habits and mistakes of misconduct relegates a person to being a victim of his errors. Letting fears inhibit progress is but another evidence of one's unwillingness to try because of the fear of failure. Roadblocks to eternal progress are cast aside when resolves are made that no man needs to walk alone. It is a happy day when we come to know that with God's help, nothing is impossible for us.

May we look to ourselves with new responsibility, new self-appreciation, higher self-image, and greater self-respect. We are children of God. We do possess God-given attributes.

Let us so live that it may be said of us, "He is well balanced. He has faith in God and in himself. He knows where he is going and how to get there. He is a good manager of himself." By doing this, it will be possible for us to better serve in the kingdom and have a greater appreciation for the thrilling declaration, "As man now is, God once was; as God now is, man may become." (Lorenzo Snow.)

LORD, INCREASE OUR FAITH

Bruce R. McConkie

Faith like that of the ancients—what we would give to possess it!

By faith all things are possible. To name the fruits of faith is simply to list all of the miracles, all of the gifts and signs, all of the events of creation, redemption, and salvation.

By faith Enoch walked with God; Melchizedek quenched the violence of fire; Moses led Israel through the Red Sea; Joshua stopped the sun; Elijah called down fire from heaven; Daniel stopped the mouths of lions; Moriancumer moved Mount Zerin; and Peter and Paul raised the dead. By faith, prophets in all ages have opened the eyes of the blind, unstopped the ears of the deaf, loosed the tongues of the dumb, healed withered limbs, rebuked diseases, restored health.

By faith, men accept the gospel, forsake the world, become the sons of God, go on to eternal perfection, and gain mansions in that kingdom where God and Christ dwell.

"Faith is . . . the moving cause of all action in . . . intelligent beings." It is a "principle . . . of power." It "is the first great governing principle which has power, dominion, and authority over all things; by it they exist, by it they are upheld, by it they are changed, or by it they remain agreeable to the will of God. Without it there is no power, and without power there could be no creation nor existence." So taught the Prophet Joseph Smith in the *Lectures on Faith*.

The ancient apostles—knowing of the mighty deeds done by the prophets who preceded them, knowing that these things had been done by faith, knowing that faith was a principle of power—presented to the Master this petition: "Increase our faith." They wanted, through faith, what every saint, ancient and modern, desires—to have power to do all things that are harmonious with the will of God in this life and then to gain eternal salvation in the life to come.

Jesus' reply (as far as the record reveals) did not answer

54

their query. Instead, He spoke simply of the transcendent power manifest through the exercise of faith. "If ye had faith as a grain of mustard seed," said He, "ye might say unto this sycamine tree, Be thou plucked up by the root, and be thou planted in the sea; and it should obey you." (Luke 17:5-6.)

And so the problem remains. As with the Twelve in Palestine, so with the saints today. How is faith gained, increased, perfected, until the man of God attains that spiritual stature which assures him of eternal life? "Lord, increase our faith."

As they petitioned, so do we pray: "Lord, let us have power to uproot sycamine trees, to move mountains, to work miracles, to do all things needful while here on earth, and to be saved in thy kingdom in due course." As they knew, so do we that faith and its fruits go together, that if we possess that power which is faith, we will enjoy those things which are the fruits of faith.

Joseph Smith said: "Because faith is wanting, the fruits are. No man since the world was had faith without having something along with it. The ancients quenched the violence of fire, escaped the edge of the sword, women received their dead, etc. By faith the worlds were made. A man who has none of the gifts has no faith; and he deceives himself, if he supposes he has. Faith has been wanting, not only among the heathen, but in professed Christendom also, so that tongues, healings, prophecy, and prophets and apostles, and all the gifts and blessings have been wanting." (*History of the Church* 5:218.)

Viewed in its proper perspective, then, the pursuit of faith becomes man's most important enterprise, for through faith men gain the greatest blessings both in time and in eternity. For the spiritual novice, the spiritually weak, the seeker who is but beginning—perhaps even for the apostles who were told anew by their Lord of the power that is faith—the casting of sycamine trees into the sea seems, if not impossible, at least a difficult thing reserved for a favored few.

And so, perhaps, it is, for faith (or power) is found in all degrees and in all quantities. One man has faith (or power) to do one thing, and another has power (or faith) to do something greater. Thus the Prophet said: "Miracles are the fruits of faith. . . . Faith comes by hearing the word of God. If a man has not faith enough to do one thing, he may have faith to do another: if he cannot remove a mountain, he may heal the sick. Where faith is there will be some of the fruits: all gifts and power which were sent from heaven, were poured out on the heads of those who had faith." (*History of the Church* 5:355.)

In gaining faith, there must be a beginning point, a place to start, a time when the power that is faith finds initial lodgment in the human soul. Since faith comes by hearing the word of God (Romans 10:17), faith seekers must hear the word of God taught, taught in plainness and perfection by legal administrators who have power and insight and who teach the truth.

Those who hear must elect to be receptive; they must make an initial choice to believe. Alma stated it this way: "If ye will awake and arouse your faculties, even to an experiment upon my words, and exercise a particle of faith, yea, even if ye can no more than desire to believe, let this desire work in you, even until ye believe in a manner that ye can give place for a portion of my words." He then compared the word unto a seed that if planted in the heart and allowed to swell and grow, would enlarge the soul and enlighten the understanding. Then he asked: "Would not this increase your faith?" (Alma 32:27-28.)

Thus Alma, in general terms, tells how to lay a foundation for gaining an increasing faith. But it is left to Joseph Smith to spell out the details, to announce the specific formula for faith. He said that "three things are necessary in order that any rational and intelligent being may exercise faith in God unto life and salvation." These he named as:

"First, the idea that he actually exists.

"Secondly, a *correct* idea of his character, perfections, and attributes.

"Thirdly, an actual knowledge that the course of life

56

which he is pursuing is according to his will." (*Lectures on Faith* 3:2-5.)

Following this perfect formula for faith will seem easy to some members of the Church, hard to others. Some of its provisions are almost automatically fulfilled by every member of the kingdom; others seemingly require a constant labor and effort.

As to the idea that God actually exists, there is no problem. From that spring morning in 1820, when the Father and the Son stood in glorious immortality before the destined head of this dispensation, there has never been any question in the minds of true Latter-day Saints as to the existence of Deity. We worship that God in whose image man is made; that holy and exalted Personage who is our Father in heaven; that Supreme Being of whom the revelation says: "The Father has a body of flesh and bones as tangible as man's; the Son also; but the Holy Ghost has not a body of flesh and bones, but is a personage of Spirit." (D&C 130:22.)

As to having a correct idea of his character, perfections, and attributes, the problem is a little more difficult.

By way of summary, the Prophet spells out the *character* of God under six headings:

"First, that he was God before the world was created, and the same God that he was after it was created.

"Secondly, that he is merciful and gracious, slow to anger, abundant in goodness, and that he was so from everlasting, and will be to everlasting.

"Thirdly, that he changes not, neither is there variableness with him; but that he is the same yesterday, to-day, and for ever; and that his course is one eternal round, without variation.

"Fourthly, that he is a God of truth and cannot lie.

"Fifthly, that he is no respecter of persons:

"Sixthly, that he is love." (*Lectures* 3:13-18.)

Most members of the Church find it easy to set their souls in harmony with these eternal truths, which taken collectively make up the character of Deity.

God's *attributes* are given as: knowledge, faith or power, justice, judgment, mercy, and truth. The Prophet explains that "without the idea of the existence of the attributes which belong to God, the minds of men could not have power to exercise faith in him so as to lay hold upon eternal life." (*Lectures* 4:2.) Here again, the members of the kingdom find little difficulty in ascribing to the Almighty the very attributes that he possesses.

"What we mean by perfections," the Prophet says, "is, the perfections which belong to all the attributes of his nature." (*Lectures* 5:1.) This means, for instance, that Deity has all mercy; that there is no part of this attribute that He must yet gain; that He is the embodiment, the personification, the total possessor of it all. It means He is not only a Being endowed with the attributes of truth and knowledge, but that He also possesses these attributes in their fulness and perfection. In other words, He knows all things and is not gaining new knowledge or learning new truths. And so it is with each attribute; the perfection of God consists in possessing them in their fulness and perfection. These concepts are not too difficult for most members of the restored kingdom, but there are some who stumble to a degree by professing to worship a progressing rather than a perfected God.

In explaining and amplifying the phase of the perfections of God deal with truth and knowledge, Joseph Smith taught:

"Without the knowledge of all things, God would not be able to save any portion of his creatures; for it is by reason of the knowledge which he has of all things, from the beginning to the end, that enables him to give that understanding to his creatures by which they are made partakers of eternal life; and if it were not for the idea existing in the minds of men that God had all knowledge it would be impossible for them to exercise faith in him." (*Lectures* 4:11.)

Now as to the third requirement in the formula for faith, that of gaining an actual knowledge that the course of one's life is according to the divine will, this is the place where the greatest obstacles are found. On this point the Prophet's language is: "An actual knowledge to any person, that the course of life which he pursues is according to the will of God, is essentially necessary to enable him to have that confidence in God without which no person can obtain eternal life." (*Lectures* 6:2.)

In other words, faith is born of righteousness; faith follows obedience; faith is the power that God gives to those who serve Him in righteousness and in truth unto the end.

What, then, is the revealed answer to the apostolic plea, "Lord, increase our faith"?

Surely it is this:

Faith comes by hearing the word of God, by accepting the apostles and prophets who represent Deity, by learning the true doctrines of salvation.

Faith comes because we let the seed of the word swell in our bosoms until light and understanding fills our souls.

Faith comes when we believe in our hearts that God actually exists, when we accept the truth as to His character, perfections, and attributes.

And, finally, faith comes, increases, and is tested as we so live as to gain the actual assurance that our lives are in harmony with the divine will. And when it comes, what glories it brings!

Hear, in conclusion, the words of the Prophet:

"When faith comes it brings its train of attendants with it—apostles, prophets, evangelists, pastors, teachers, gifts, wisdom, knowledge, miracles, healings, tongues, interpretation of tongues, etc. All these appear when faith appears on the earth, and disappear when it disappears from the earth; for these are the effects of faith, and always have attended, and always will, attend it. For where faith is, there will the knowledge of God be also, with all things which pertain thereto—revelations, visions, and dreams, as well as every necessary thing, in order that the possessors of faith may be perfected, and obtain salvation; for God must change, otherwise faith will prevail with him. And he who possesses it will, through it obtain all necessary knowledge and wisdom, until he shall know God, and the Lord Jesus Christ, whom he has sent—whom to know is eternal life." (*Lectures* 7:20.)

BUILD
YOUR SHIELD
OF FAITH

Elder L. Tom Perry

I was reared in a home in which parents loved and appreciated the gospel of Jesus Christ. They understood the admonition of Paul to the Ephesian saints when he wrote, "Finally, my brethren, be strong in the Lord, and in the power of his might. Put on the whole armour of God, that ye may be able to stand against the wiles of the devil. Stand therefore, having your loins girt about with truth, and having on the breastplate of righteousness; and your feet shod with the preparation of the gospel of peace; above all, taking the shield of faith, wherewith ye shall be able to quench all the fiery darts of the wicked." (Ephesians 6:10-11, 14-16.)

We were dressed in our home each morning not only with hats and raincoats and boots to protect us from physical storm, but even more carefully in the armor of God. As we would kneel in family prayer and listen to our father, a bearer of the priesthood, pour out his soul to the Lord for the protection of his family against the fiery darts of the wicked, one more layer was added to our shield of faith. While our shield was being made strong, theirs was always available, for they were available, and we knew it.

What a protection it is to travel through the journey of life knowing that a shield of faith is being carefully constructed for us by loving parents from our first moments on earth.

Let me just give you a small example of how that shield would work. One day I was made an attractive offer by a group of marines, buddies of mine, as we were about to go on liberty. It wasn't until after we were on our way that I discovered this was not the best of company to be in. It was then that I found out the reason they had invited me. It was because they knew of my standards. They knew that I would be sober when it was time to return to the base, and I could guide them back.

We found ourselves in Los Angeles on a streetcar headed toward a dance hall. They had already started to drink a little, and I was ready to part company with them. Then that protective shield took over, and I knew of the prayers of my parents for my welfare. The streetcar stopped and allowed new passengers to come aboard. The new passengers separated me from my buddies and pushed me to the back of the car. There I discovered a nice group of young people standing and seated. Immediately upon finding me in their company, one spoke up and said, "Hi, Marine! We're Mormons. What do you know about our church?"

I answered, "Plenty," and got off the streetcar with them and went to a ward social.

The shield of faith was there. It was protecting me from the fiery darts of the wicked in order that in a proper time in my life I would be worthy to take an angel into the temple of the Lord, and there at its altar we would be sealed together for time and all eternity.

I know by personal experience the value of having noble parents to build around their children a protective shield of faith in our Lord and our Savior Jesus Christ. I give you my witness that it works. May every child of God be given that opportunity in their lives—to start each day having their fathers blessing their home and giving them that protective shield of faith as they depart from the home to go about their every activity.

FAITHFUL
SERVANTS

Elder J. Thomas Fyans

During the existence of this world, when there has been need, the Lord has spoken to a faithful servant. The dictionary tells us that *faithful* means "full of faith, true in affection or allegiance." What kind of person is a faithful servant of the Lord? Where do we find instances of faithful servants?

In the scriptures we find many examples. Noah responded to the direction he received from heaven. He built an ark and placed aboard it all that he was commanded to. "Thus did Noah; according to all that God commanded him, so did he." Then the Lord said to Noah, "Come thou and all thy house into the ark; for thee have I seen righteousness before me in this generation." Noah, being full of faith, saved himself and his family. (Genesis 6:22; 7:1.)

In the Book of Mormon, we read: "Behold I, Nephi, will show unto you that the tender mercies of the Lord are over all those whom he hath chosen, because of their faith, to make them mighty even unto the power of deliverance." (1 Nephi 1:20.)

Then Nephi describes the deliverance of his father and family: "For behold, it came to pass that the Lord spake unto my father, yea, even in a dream, and said unto him: Blessed art thou Lehi, because of the things which thou hast done; and because thou hast been faithful and declared unto this people the things which I commanded thee, behold, they seek to take away thy life.

"And it came to pass that the Lord commanded my father, even in a dream, that he should take his family and depart into the wilderness." (1 Nephi 1:20; 2:1-2.)

Many other instances are recorded in the holy writ, such as Abraham and Moses receiving inspirational direction so that they and their loved ones might avoid destruction.

Inspiration from heaven does not always require a physical move. In fact, it more frequently requires a spiritual move, from an undesirable condition to one more compatible with the Spirit of the Lord. All of these moves, spiritual and physical, require faith.

The scriptures give us instances of faith in centuries past. Let us look at an instance within a few years of today. When the First Presidency and the Council of the Twelve of the Church directed that the Translation Department become functional in the Orient, the General Authorities and mission presidents were asked whom they would recommend to assume this very important key role. This man needed to be a person who was full of faith. The name of Kan Watanabe was recommended by several. In Tokyo, an interview was arranged with Brother Watanabe, and as we awaited his arrival, Elder Adney Komatsu, an Assistant to the Council of the Twelve now, but president of the Japan Mission in Tokyo then, recounted this story as a basis for his recommendation of Brother Watanabe.

Brother Watanabe was serving as a counselor to President Komatsu in the Japan Mission. One day in a conversation with Brother Watanabe, President Komatsu said, "Because you live several hundred miles from here, I sometimes feel that I am in a boxing ring and have one hand tied behind me." This statement was meant to compliment Brother Watanabe and recognize his contribution to the presidency of the mission.

Not long after this comment had been made, Brother Watanabe appeared at the mission headquarters in Tokyo and said to President Komatsu, "Here I am." President Komatsu replied, "Yes, I see you." Brother Watanabe then said, "No, what I am saying is that I am now here in Tokyo. I have left my employment and have moved my family, and I am now here so that you will be in a boxing ring with both hands ready. One hand will not be tied behind you." What a display of faith! Brother Watanabe soon found a very fine position that would allow him to take care of his family temporally.

As Brother Watanabe was ushered into a room for the interview and we described to him the responsibility that would evolve upon the shoulders of the person charged with the responsibility of translating, printing, and distributing materials in the Orient, we asked, "Would you like to assume this responsibility?" He responded immediately, "If that is what the Lord would like me to do, I am ready." He left his employment and began this new assignment immediately. He was willing to accept the direction of the Lord.

Faith gives us the assurance that we can expect to attain a certain result if we act in a particular way. If we wish to leave a room, we will get up and move toward the particular exit that will allow us to arrive at the desired destination. In turning out a light, we will automatically use the switch that we believe controls that certain light. We learn from new experiences, but we rarely move in a direction unless faith gives us the feeling that we can thereby accomplish a desired goal. Faith is a condition of the heart and mind, built on experience, that gives us the motivation to move ahead in all areas of our lives.

Lasting faith must be built on true principles, and the process of building faith is the testing of knowledge for its truth. Faith increases as our knowledge increases, but the degree of faith depends upon the intensity and certainty of our belief. Great faith can even accompany limited knowledge; it has great motivating power.

Our wise Father in heaven desires us to build strength within ourselves, and He does this by giving us free agency and allowing us to choose for ourselves.

President Joseph Fielding Smith said: "Wouldn't it be easy for the Lord to have an angel come in the midst of heaven and cry to all people everywhere upon the face of the earth and tell them that Joseph Smith was a prophet of God? That is not His way of doing. We came here to this world to be tried and proved to see what kind of stuff we are made of, and to walk by faith."

The principle of faith is probably the basic principle of all human life, and it is the first principle of the gospel of Jesus Christ. The basic saving principle is faith in Jesus as the

Christ. We need a great faith in Jesus as the Son of God, in His atoning sacrifice for all mankind, and in the fact that obeying His commandments will place us on the road to eternal life. The reward for faith will come when we demonstrate it by our works.

How can faith motivate us in our daily lives? It can give us a positive approach to living. Because of the promises from the Lord, we should be willing to keep our bodies clean and in good physical condition. In view of our covenant and promise, through baptism and partaking of the sacrament, to follow the gospel plan by keeping the commandments, we should have no problem in being honest and upright in all of our dealings with our fellowmen and in giving faithful and devoted service in our church assignments. Faith will give us the desire to improve ourselves by gaining more knowledge and by developing talents and skills that will help us to have greater ability in every facet of our lives. We will grow spiritually as we are motivated to stay in communication with our Heavenly Father through prayer, to read the scriptures, to listen to the counsel of our latter-day prophets, and to live in such a way as to have the Holy Ghost as our companion.

We are continually faced with decisions. Daily we have to decide where we are going and by what route we will reach the desired goal. One day a father was backing his car in an abandoned lot. His little daughter, who was riding with him, said, "Daddy, you are getting into a hole." The father did not pay any attention and kept backing until her insistent cry caused him to apply the brakes and drive forward. His heart sank when he saw a large pit covered with rotting boards and the tire marks just about a foot from having backed into a real problem.

He said, "Suppose I had not believed her. All of my superior wisdom, my determination, my stubbornness for believing that I was always right all argued against my faith in her sure knowledge. The insistence in her tone of voice rather than my faith in her word finally made me alter my course."

Is this the way we react to the warnings we receive from our Heavenly Father through His servants as they say "Stop, you are backing into a problem that may lead you from the straight and narrow way; change your direction"? Do we have the faith to listen to the servants of God and to follow their counsel that we should obey all of His commandments? If we have such faith, we can be sure that God will keep His promises to us. We will find the right course and will be rewarded with happy, successful lives here, and we can look forward to eternal lives in the hereafter.

FAITH IN THE LIVES
OF THE SAINTS

Elder M. Russell Ballard

What a priceless collection of faith-promoting experiences can be found in the scriptures! I marvel at the powerful accounts they contain:

The aged patriarch Abraham ascending Mount Moriah with his only son Isaac.

A young shepherd boy challenging the giant of the Philistine armies.

Alma and Amulek imprisoned at Ammonihah.

You and I are constantly nourished by these great examples of faith and miracles from the past.

But what of today? As the prophet Mormon asked: "Has the day of miracles ceased? Or have angels ceased to appear unto the children of men? Or has he withheld the power of the Holy Ghost from them? Or will he, so long as time shall last, or the earth shall stand, or there shall be one man upon the face thereof to be saved? Behold I say unto you, Nay; for it is by faith that miracles are wrought." (Moroni 7:35-37.)

Yes, faith is the key. And as I travel over the Church, I find such miracle-spawning faith to be in abundant supply. I agree with President Heber J. Grant, who said: "I bear my witness to you that if a record had been made of all those who have been afflicted, those who have been given up to die, and who have been healed by the power of God, since the establishment of the Church of Christ in our day, it would make a book much larger than the New Testament. More miracles have been performed in the Church of Jesus Christ of Latter-day Saints than we have any account of in the days of the Savior and His Apostles. Today, sickness is cured by spiritual power. . . . The dead have been raised. My own brother was announced to be dead, but by the prayer of faith he lives and presides over one of the stakes of Zion. I know, as I know I live, that the healing power of Almighty

God . . . is in the Church of Christ of which you and I are members." (*Conference Report,* October 6, 1910, p. 119.)

May I take you on a globe-spanning tour to show you the faith that exists today in the lives of Latter-day Saints?

Our first stop is New Zealand. It is March 1976, and the Saints of this South Pacific island are anxiously preparing for their first area conference and the arrival of President Spencer W. Kimball. President Kimball had just concluded a rigorous schedule of conference sessions in Samoa. Between sessions he had selflessly exposed himself to all manner of sickness as he gave blessings to numerous people who sought his aid. Then, shortly afterward, he himself was stricken with a serious illness, similar to the type he had rebuked in several administrations. Both he and Sister Kimball had temperatures of 104 degrees. They were coughing, violently nauseated, and most miserable.

Russell M. Nelson, the prophet's attending physician, recalled that President Kimball was "gray and ashen" as he and D. Arthur Haycock, President Kimball's secretary, assisted him onto the airplane for the flight to New Zealand. One official scolded Dr. Nelson for allowing President Kimball to get on the plane, saying "Anyone can see that he's too sick to get on an airplane and fly to New Zealand. You should leave him here in Pago Pago, where he can go to the hospital and get the aid that he needs." Nevertheless President and Sister Kimball were settled on the plane with blankets while their fevers raged between 102 and 104 degrees.

In New Zealand President and Sister Kimball were rushed to the home of the temple president, and they immediately went to bed. President Kimball asked President N. Eldon Tanner to handle the planned reception with the Maori queen, since he himself was too ill to go. Moreover, he said, "Sister Kimball and I will not make it to the cultural activities planned for this evening because of our illness. The doctor thinks we should not attend. Therefore, will you please excuse us and begin the meeting on time. Express our regrets to the congregation. We will try to conserve our strength in order to make it to the general sessions of the area conference tomorrow morning." President Tanner agreed and left.

Dr. Nelson remained with President and Sister Kimball while his wife, Dantzel, went with the other Brethren and their wives to the stadium at the Church College of New Zealand for the cultural program. All was quiet at the temple president's home while the prophet and his wife slept. Brother Nelson recalls what happened then:

I was reading in President Kimball's room when he awakened with a start.

He said, "Brother Nelson, what time was that program to begin this evening?"

I said, "At seven o'clock, President Kimball."

He said, "What time is it now?"

I replied, "It's almost seven." Noting that he was soaked in perspiration, I thought his fever may have broken, which indeed it had. His temperature was now 98.6 degrees.

He said, "Tell Sister Kimball we're going!"

Several thoughts flashed through my mind in that instant, culminating in a decision that it would be inadvisable for me to say anything about it being medically inadvisable for him to go. So I quickly went in and said to Sister Kimball, "We're going." They each hurriedly prepared and went to the car that had been made available.

So President and Sister Kimball, Brother Haycock, and I drove the short distance from the temple president's home to the Church College stadium, where the activities were being held. As the car entered the stadium, there was a very loud shout that erupted spontaneously. It was so sudden and so deafening that I wondered if it might have been a clap of thunder. The car was driven around the track to the place where President and Sister Kimball could be ushered to their seats; Brother Haycock and I took our seats beside our companions as well. I asked Dantzel what was the cause of that enormous shout. I got the story from her point of view.

She said that President Tanner had called the meeting to order at 7:00 P.M. and had explained that President and Sister Kimball were unable to attend because of illness. They were to proceed without them in order that their strength might be preserved to join with the Saints the following day. Then one of the young New Zealanders was called upon to pray. With a faith typical to these Saints in the islands, this young New Zealander gave what my wife described as a rather lengthy prayer. During the course of his prayer, he supplicated the Lord thusly: "We are three thousand New Zealand youth. We are assembled here, having prepared for six months to sing and to dance for thy prophet. Wilt thou heal him and deliver him here." Then, as the "Amen" was pronounced, the car entered carrying President and Sister Kimball. They were immediately identified by the assembled throng of thousands, who all spontaneously issued that shout for joy on having their prayer answered so directly." (Russell M. Nelson, *From Heart to Heart, An Autobiography*, 1979, pp. 177-80.)

Missionary work is one area where faith and their attendant miracles are particularly evident in our day.

Several years ago, I was assigned to supervise missionary work and other Church work in the southeastern part of the United States. In that capacity I had the great opportunity to meet with missionaries in zone conferences. While sitting on the stand in a zone conference at one time in the Columbia South Carolina Mission, I noticed a missionary and his companion come in, walk across the back of the hall, and come down the aisle. Then I watched as the senior companion, with great empathy and love, gently arranged for the seating of his junior companion. As I watched, I turned to President Ronald Knighton and inquired, "Is that elder blind?" Upon learning that he was, I confessed to President Knighton, "I didn't know that we sent totally blind young men or women on full-time missions."

I had a great spiritual experience as I met that young man, Elder Nolan Crabb, after the meeting. I embraced him and told him how proud I was of him and how sure I was that the Lord was blessing him. He served a glorious mission surrounded by physical darkness, but filled to overflowing with the spirit of the gospel and the light of the Lord. He touched many, many lives. No missionary who served in that mission brought more people into the Church than did this young man. He served as zone leader and finished his mission as the assistant to the president of the mission, despite his blindness.

Upon arriving home from his mission, he was called into his bishop's office in Ogden, Utah, and given a very special blessing. Three months later, he was at Brigham Young University, white cane in hand, learning his way from one building to another. With the help of a mobility instructor he was able to learn 95 to 98 percent of the campus.

One day, while Nolan was in a hurry to get to a class, a friend came along and said, "I'll take you with me." As they were running along, his friend took a shortcut through an area Nolan had never been through before. Then his friend stopped in the middle and said, "I've got to take off to my class now, but you can make it; it's really easy." Nolan was left alone. He said it was like being flown over to Tokyo, dropped out of the plane, and told, "Walk to the temple site." But Nolan began to move, and as he did so, he said, "Now, Father, the nearest person is about three hundred feet away, and this is BYU, where you don't ruin your reputation by hollering, 'Hey, come and help.' People would think I was some kind of a freak, and I couldn't afford that. So you're the only one who can hear me at this point. Can you please get me out of this jam? I'm not exactly sure where I am." As he started to move again, he began to hear a voice, clear and distinct, that said "Turn left here," or "Go right," or "Stay straight." He also felt a hand on his shoulder, and so real was that force and feeling that he turned around to see who was there. He obviously did not see anyone, but more significantly, he did not hear any footsteps either, nor did anyone speak. Within two minutes, he heard the sound of a familiar landmark. Sensing his location, he was able to turn and enter the building where his class was.

There were tears in his eyes as the Spirit recalled from his memory the words of his bishop in the blessing he gave him three months earlier after his mission: "I bless you that in your time of trial the angels of God will come and encamp round about you. And though they will be unseen, they will serve as your guiding lights, as your beacons, and as your friends to guide you in areas throughout this earth wherein you need their help."

Yes, angels, healings, gifts of the Spirit, and other miracles operate daily in the lives of faithful Latter-day Saints who have committed themselves to the service of the Lord and their fellowmen. Even the tempering of the elements is possible when faith is strong enough and the Lord requires it. I was thrilled in general conference a few years ago to hear Douglas W. DeHaan, president of the Portland Oregon East Stake, tell of such an experience:

The Portland Oregon East Stake has been developing a dairy farm over the past half dozen years or more. It is located on an island in the Columbia River and is one of the largest single-stake projects in the Church. This fact, coupled with the need to develop the project almost from scratch, has placed a heavy burden upon our people, both in time and in money.

With a new project, we had run in the red each year, but 1977 was to be our turnabout year. The final result depended upon harvesting about seventy-five acres of corn, which was to be made into silage for feed. Unseasonably, it had rained almost every day during the month of September, and by the first day of October, our scheduled harvest date, I knew the crop was in trouble. We have a very high water table on the island, and when the ground gets saturated with too much water we get so much mud our harvest equipment cannot get into the fields without sinking. Once the land is saturated it takes about a month of dry weather to make the fields passable to vehicles. During the winter months and right up until June, the corn ground is entirely under water.

I visit the farm about once a week, so I keep a pair of rubber boots in my car. I drove to the farm that October day and decided to pull on my boots and walk down into the corn fields. I immediately found even the road turned to mud and puddles. In places the mud came near the top of my eighteen-inch-high boots, and I don't really know why I continued walking. It was a dark gray, overcast day, and drops of rain were splashing in the open puddles everywhere. The farm crew told me they had taken a corn chopper down into the fields a few days earlier but had it down to the axles in mud somewhere in the long corn rows.

As I walked I noticed that the corn itself was a fine crop, with row after row ten to fourteen feet high. Now, I rarely get depressed, but I was feeling really low that day. I knew how hard everyone had worked and what it meant to lose that fine crop. I eventually came to the spot where the chopper had gone in, and looking way down the rows I saw it sunk deep into the mud. For some reason I decided to walk to the chopper, and as I entered the rows and splashed on through the mud and water, I was startled to hear a voice. I am sure that the voice came to me only in my mind, but I could hear the voice and admonition of President Kimball. He said softly, "Is anything too hard for the Lord?" (Genesis 18:14.) Now, like you, I have heard him say that many times, but I did not fully focus upon it before this time. I smiled to myself and said, "Yes, President, I believe this mess may be too hard even for the Lord."

As I neared the chopper, I was impressed to climb up on it and upon doing so found my head was about two feet above seventy-five acres of that tall, splendid corn. As I looked about in discouragement, the voice seemed to come to me again, but this time in a more serious tone, "President, is there anything too hard for the Lord?" At once I felt ashamed of my attitude of depression, and soon I was no longer looking down but up into the sky. Before I realized it, I was talking, yes, pleading aloud with the Lord in faith. When I had finished, I had committed that crop and the harvesting of it into the hands of the Lord and had done so by the power of the priesthood of God. I recall that as I climbed down from the chopper, tears were still streaming from my eyes. I grew concerned as I slowly walked away considering what it was that I had just done. Yet I knew that I had done it in total faith, that there was a proper need, and that it was a righteous request of the Lord.

Because of the spiritual nature of my experience, I think I had decided not to tell anyone of it. But the very next Sunday I was sitting on the stand during one of our ward sacrament meetings. I was not scheduled to speak, but the bishop got up with about ten minutes remaining and said, "I feel President DeHaan has had a spiritual experience that he needs to share with us." I got up reluctantly, knowing what it was I had to relate. I did so and asked the congregation to join me with their faith. Now, we have Saints with great testimonies in our stake, and my experience spread rapidly throughout the wards. I learned several weeks later that members were even telling their nonmember friends to go ahead and plan picnics and outdoor activities, because even in Oregon it was not going to rain throughout October. On the day following my experience in the corn fields, the sun came out for the first time in nearly thirty days. Then the next day we had sun, and the day following that. Before long the temperature was back into the high seventies. Every day for the next three weeks the weather forecast called for rain, but each day no rain fell.

I recall that about two weeks later I flew to Seattle, about two hundred miles to the north, on business. It rained very hard there all day, and as I made the return trip to Portland it rained all the way until we reached the Columbia River, which surrounds our farm. Miraculously, the clouds parted and the rain ceased. That day I cut a little weather map from the newspaper showing the rain ending at the river and put it on our refrigerator as a reminder to keep my faith. Three weeks after my original experience in the fields, I drove to the farm once again. I put on my boots and went back into the corn. This time the ground was soft but firming. That was on a Friday, and our fine farm crew was already making plans to begin the harvest on the following Monday.

That same day an acquaintance of mine from a local television station called. He said, "I understand the Mormons are developing a fine dairy farm on Sauvies Island." I answered in the affirmative, and he inquired, "Is there a story there?" I told him there was, but I knew he could never capture the *real* story. That very Monday, as we began our harvest, we had a camera crew on the farm for several hours, and we did get some fine publicity for the Church.

With the loyal assistance of many of the members, we worked day and night for the next five days. By the following Saturday, all of the freshly chopped corn was safely in our silage pits, and we finished covering it over with plastic. At last we had the feed needed to get us through the winter. Within an hour after having covered the crop, the heavens just seemed to open and commenced one of the heaviest and longest downpours I can remember. The fields from which the corn had just been removed were flooded and remained under water from that day until the following June. As I stood in the rain with feelings of gratitude that I'll never be able to adequately describe, it seemed to me that the Lord had just saved it up until our spiritual understanding had been fulfilled. (*Ensign*, November 1980, pp. 87-88.)

Our Church leaders have faith-promoting experiences almost daily. I was privileged to participate in such an incident on a Fast Sunday recently when I had the pleasure of being in my own ward. A young sister arose to bear her testimony. I had known her father for many years and knew that he was presently on a Church assignment away from Salt Lake City. As she bore her testimony, she talked about the tremendous difficulties her older sister was undergoing in a pregnancy. She was bearing her testimony essentially for the faith of the ward to help her older sister. As I sat listening to her remarks, the impression hit me that I must go and give the sister a blessing.

Later in the day, my wife and I went to the home of the older sister. A member of her family answered our knock. He hesitated to let us in because of the physical appearance of the bedridden, expectant mother. She had contracted shingles, her face was a mass of scabs, and she looked as though she had been in a terrible fight. It was understandable that she didn't want to see anyone.

Being a devout member of the Church, this young mother had always desired to do what the Lord wanted her to do. She had always felt that her mission was to bring children into the world. But in prior pregnancies she had had severe complications, so it was understandable that she had fears, anxieties, and worries over this pregnancy.

I was prompted by the Spirit to tell the family that I had been directed there by the Lord to give her a blessing. With that message, she came into the room, and there, with the help of her husband and her father-in-law, I gave her a blessing. As I sealed the anointing, words flowed and promises were made that were frightening. I even wanted to hold back, but it didn't seem right to do that. The impression came to let her know that I was standing there, not only as her neighbor and as a General Authority, but as a proxy for her absent father. When those words slipped from my lips and fell upon the head of this daughter, she wept. We were all weeping.

The following Wednesday, she had an appointment with her doctor. Much to her relief and with a heart full of gratitude, she learned that all of her bodily functions had returned to normal, the afflictions to her face and body had receded, and her general well-being had returned. I had occasion to see her a short time after that, and what a blessing it was to see this sweet sister, who had been so very sick, bedridden, and unable to move, up and about and doing so very well. A few weeks later she brought her little infant son, who was born normal and well and healthy in every way, for us to see.

Because of experiences like this that come into my life, it is easy for me to bear testimony that I know that the Church is true, that I know that Jesus is the Christ, that this is His work, and that our Heavenly Father is very close to us.

I know that the faith of righteous individuals is a very real force in the universe. It is the key that unlocks the heavens and allows the Almighty to pour down knowledge, blessings, and even miracles upon the heads of the Latter-day Saints. I testify that the faith of the ancients is with us today and is manifested in the lives of humble people throughout the world.

IN DEFENSE
OF FAITH

Elder Theodore M. Burton

When I was a small child, my mother taught me colors. She held up a blue-colored object and told me it was blue. Then she had me repeat the word after her. After a while she would hold another object before my eyes and ask me its color.

"Green?" I asked.

"No, dear," she replied patiently, "this color is blue."

"Blue?" I questioned.

"Yes, dear. This color is blue."

After a while she held up another blue-colored object and asked me its color.

"Yellow?" I questioned.

"No, love, not yellow." Then even more patiently she taught me, "This color is blue."

"Blue," I echoed.

"Yes, dear," she repeated, "this color is blue."

She let me play a while and then held up another blue-colored object and asked, "What color is this?"

"Blue?" I queried.

"That's my smart boy!" Mother proudly replied, and she gave me a big hug and a kiss. So I learned to know colors.

I have no idea how long it took my patient mother to teach me colors. I wasn't any smarter or any slower than other boys. But eventually I learned to distinguish blue from other colors. Now when anyone holds up such an object and asks me what color it is, I confidently answer, "Blue!" If anyone should ask me what makes me think that color is blue, I answer, "I *know* it is blue, for I can *see* it!" Others agree with me, for they too can see that it is blue. The object, however, is blue only because we agree with one another to call such a color blue. In other words, everything we say we know is only because we had been taught it. Our knowledge comes from those things we have been taught or have read or have heard or have experienced.

Later on I became a student in college, and I found that some of the things I believed in and felt I knew to be true were regarded as ridiculous and immature to some of my professors. They believed in things totally foreign to the beliefs I had been taught from my earliest childhood. They ridiculed my belief in God as simply superstitious nonsense. They made fun of the Book of Mormon. They laughed at the concept of Joseph Smith being a prophet. They refused to believe the Bible was anything more than literature. I felt crushed.

To me these were learned men. They held doctor's degrees from great universities. They were well-read. They seemed to have answers and proofs for everything they taught. I was merely a student, and they were professors with years of schooling, research knowledge, and experience. To say that I was impressed is perhaps an understatement. My faith and my beliefs were shaken, and I teetered on the edge of an abyss of indecision. What should I accept as truth? Should I accept the teachings of these learned men, or should I retain my belief in what I had been taught by my parents, my Sunday School, Primary, religion class, and priesthood teachers, and had learned through my own experiences?

I now have my own doctor's degree in a field of exact science. I received that degree from a great midwestern university. I have also taught at another fine university as a full professor of chemistry. I have done research on my own and have directed students in original scientific inquiry. I know enough about science now to appreciate the difference between what we call fact and theory. I know from study and personal experience the degree of faith involved in even the most precise areas of scientific knowledge. I know the limits of so-called laws and recognize their value and practical use. The knowledge of my former teachers was often based on theories that have not been proven without question even at this late date. They accepted as fact things that were neither proven nor verified. But I did not know these things when I was a student.

I shudder when I think of those days. How easily I could have followed those teachers, who were most sincere in their beliefs. How easily I could have lost my faith and my standing in the Church by embracing man-made theories as truth. I would not care to live my life over again unless I could have the degree of knowledge and experience I now possess.

How grateful I am to have had goodly parents. They were happy, wonderful people. They loved us children and we loved them. I had a happy and secure childhood. I had a wonderful bishop during those critical years and a great stake president who later became president of the Church. Above all I had a kind and patient father who gave me personal encouragement and understanding help. I also had some great and good professors at the university who encouraged me to keep the faith. I noticed that these people were happy and successful, as were my own parents and religious leaders. Some of these professors became stalwart Church leaders. One of them became an apostle of the Lord Jesus Christ. Other professors and teachers were fine Christians, devout in their service to others and firm in their own belief and trust in God.

Those teachers who would have led me to reject God and my religious ideals were not always happy persons. Some were disillusioned and some were bitter. Fortunately I made my decision to stand for what I felt was truth. To one professor who was particularly sarcastic toward my religious concepts I simply stated, "Doctor, I refuse to believe you! I will answer your examination questions the way you want me to, but I want you to know that unlearned as I am, one thing I do know is that God lives. I believe in Him with all my heart. I will listen to your teachings, but I refuse to change my beliefs or my faith." He just looked at me and shook his head. But I had been a missionary, and I could not deny those things I felt deep within my heart to be true. I could not prove them to *him*, but *I* believed them, and they gave me both hope and comfort.

Just as I learned from Mother that blue is blue, so I learned from her and from my father that God is God. They taught me faith, and I believed. I am now a special witness of the divinity of Jesus Christ and of the restoration of the power of the priesthood of God. That knowledge did not come all at once. Often it came painfully and slowly, but step by step I learned through faith and prayer and by study and experience to know that God lives and that He does speak through modern prophets.

If at times you are discouraged and do not know which way to turn or what to believe, lean a little on the shoulders of my generation until you have time to know for yourselves the truth of these things. Remember that if you seek the Lord, you will find Him. Have faith in Him, and you will never be led astray. You will be happy as you grow older that you have kept the faith. You are a special generation placed on the earth by a loving God to light the lamp of hope for others who need leaders to guide them during these difficult times. God bless you, every one, to know that you *are* children of God.

BUILDING
BRIDGES
TO FAITH

Elder Loren C. Dunn

We have been referred to as a believing people. Certainly individual faith is the foundation stone of the gospel and the quality that is most important to us as individuals.

Joseph Smith said, "Faith is the assurance which men have of the existence of things which they have not seen, and the principle of action in all intelligent beings. . . . [It] is the first great governing principle." (*Lectures on Faith* 1:9, 24.)

And Jacob taught that the Lord commands all men that they must have "perfect faith in the Holy One of Israel, or they cannot be saved in the kingdom of God." (2 Nephi 9:23.)

As a principle of power and of action and as the key to our salvation, our individual faith, then, becomes of absolute importance to us.

Paul admonished us to be "an example of the believers, in word, in conversation, in charity, in spirit, in faith, in purity." (1 Timothy 4:12.)

"If ye can no more than desire to believe," said Alma, "let this desire work in you, even until ye believe in a manner that ye can give place for a portion of my words." (Alma 32:27.)

Moroni says, "Dispute not because ye see not, for ye receive no witness until after the trial of your faith." (Ether 12:6.)

There are many steps a person can take to develop the gift and power of faith. I would like to suggest six of these steps.

1. *Faith is the ability to recognize the Lord as all-powerful and the giver of all blessings.*

As King Benjamin put it: "Believe in God; believe that he is, and that he created all things, both in heaven and in earth; believe that he has all wisdom, and all power, both in heaven and in earth; believe that man doth not comprehend all things which the Lord can comprehend." (Mosiah 4:9.)

Sometimes we compartmentalize. We pray about one thing and worry about something else. We seem to limit the ability of the Lord to help us in every aspect of our lives.

John A. Widtsoe tells us the following: "For several years, under a Federal grant with my staff of workers we had gathered thousands of data in the field of soil moisture; but I could not extract any general law running through them. I gave up at last. My wife and I went to the temple that day to forget the failure. In the third endowment room, out of the unseen, came the solution, which has long since gone into print." (*In Sunlit Land: The Autobiography of John A. Widtsoe,* Salt Lake City: Milton R. Hunter and G. Homer Durham, 1952, p. 177.)

Faith, then, is the realization that the Lord can help us with all things.

2. *Faith is the ability to do what we are prompted to do, and when we are prompted to do it.*

A few years ago when we were presiding over the Sydney Mission, I was earnestly seeking a blessing from the Lord. The mission had done well but was pausing on a plateau, and we needed to move ahead once again.

On one particular day I was fasting and praying that the Lord would lead us to a new level of achievement. In the midst of my prayers came the clear impression to seek out my son and give him a blessing. I followed the prompting and found my son, whom I am close to, in another part of the house, attending to his high school studies.

I said, "How are things going?"

He answered, in typical teenage fashion, "Why?"

Not knowing what else to say, I asked, "Do you want a blessing?"

He looked at me in stunned silence for a few seconds and then said, "Yes."

The inspiration that followed from that blessing proved to be of great importance to both my son and me. It was an experience that neither of us will forget. Yet this would have been lost had I stopped to question why the Lord was turning me to my first responsibility, my family, when I was seeking a blessing for the mission.

3. *Faith is the ability to live the laws of God that control the blessings we are in need of.*

While we should not keep the commandments just to receive blessings, nevertheless, the blessings are there. President Harold B. Lee told an experience of praying very hard for a material blessing he needed badly. He stated that one day while he was praying for this blessing, he remembered that he had recently received some income that he had not yet tithed. It was as if, he said, the accusing voice of the Lord was saying: You want a blessing from me but you have not been obedient to the laws upon which such blessings are based. He said that he went and paid the tithing on that income, and then he again sought that particular blessing of the Lord. (Address delivered at Brigham Young University, June 28, 1955.)

4. *Faith is the ability to act "as if."*

In his teachings, Paul said: "By faith Noah, being warned of God of things not seen . . . prepared an ark to the saving of his house." (Hebrews 11:7.)

Many years ago during the dark days of World War II, Elvon W. Orme, the president of the Australia Mission, was invited to a faithful widow's house for Sunday dinner. Rationing had taken its toll, and many of the good foods had long since disappeared from the shelves of the local stores.

When President Orme arrived, he was shocked to find a table filled with foods that were in short supply and had not been seen for months.

"I can't eat this," he said, almost embarrassed that he was taking it out of the mouth of a widow.

"I'm afraid you'll have to," she said. "You see, I listened to the Brethren years ago and put in my year's supply, and this is the only kind of food I have."

She showed the faith to act "as if" by storing food, and the faith produced a miracle in the time of need.

I wonder how many Saints will be able to withstand the disaster of their own personal flood by showing faith in the advice of modern prophets and building an ark of family preparedness.

5. *Faith is the ability to be charitable and to believe in people.*

The Savior of the world is the foremost example of this love. After having been rejected and despised, He asked His Father to forgive those who crucified Him because "they know not what they do." (Luke 23:34.)

Joseph Smith is another example. After living a life filled with trials and betrayals, he said as he was going to Carthage: "I am going like a lamb to the slaughter, but . . . I have a conscience void of offense toward . . . all men." (*History of the Church* 6:555.)

I knew a man once whom I respected very much and who had this quality. On one occasion, a beggar came from out of town and appeared at his door and asked for money. My friend said, "I have an old barn that needs painting. If you want to paint it, I'll pay you for it." They went out to look at the barn, and then the man was sent to England's paint store and arrangements were made for him to pick up the paint he needed.

The barn was painted, and the man was paid and left town. Shortly after, Mr. England called my friend and said that the man had picked up far more paint than was needed to paint the barn. In short, my friend had been taken. Yet he took the opportunity to teach his sons a lesson. "Had I known what he did, I would have stopped him," he said. "But we have our painted barn, and the painter, whatever his problems, will always know that there was someone willing to believe in him."

Faith cannot be nourished in a heart that has been made hard by continued cynicism, skepticism, and unforgiveness. A person who cannot see the good in people not only destroys his own faith, but also becomes a basically unhappy person.

6. *Faith is the ability to allow ourselves to be guided by the priesthood.*

83

Paul teaches us this important truth: "And he [the Lord] gave some, apostles; and some, prophets; and some, evangelists; and some, pastors and teachers." And here he tells us why these priesthood leaders have been given to the Saints: "till we all come in the unity of the faith, and of the knowledge of the Son of God, unto a perfect man, unto the measure of the stature of the fulness of Christ." (Ephesians 4:11, 13.)

Priesthood leaders—all leaders who have been called by revelation under the hands of the priesthood—have been given to us so we can come to a unity of the faith, to the end that we might know the Savior and have his image in our countenance and become like him, "that every man might speak in the name of God the Lord, even the Savior of the world." (D&C 1:20.)

Years ago, President Joseph Fielding Smith, then a member of the Council of the Twelve, attended a stake conference where a relatively new stake president had been called. A man repeatedly came up to President Smith and asked him for counsel concerning a personal matter. Finally President Smith said he would see the man, provided the new stake president could be there. As the man unfolded his situation, the stake president was prompted with what the person needed to do. Yet President Smith listened to the brother and surprised everyone by saying, "I have no counsel for you." The man was surprised, and he left. After he had gone, President Smith turned to the stake president and said, "I knew how to counsel that man, but I was also prompted to know that he would go against the counsel. So rather than condemn him for going against the counsel of the priesthood, I told him nothing."

From this we learn that it is not enough to seek the direction of those whom God has called to lead us. We must also come with a willingness to follow the counsel of inspired leaders in order to develop our faith.

Latter-day Saints need to believe. They need to take every opportunity to develop faith, both in their own lives and in the lives of others. Faith is a part of our heritage. Those who embrace the gospel of Jesus Christ are the blood of Israel, and characteristic of the house of Israel is the ability to believe. Some have referred to it as "believing blood."

My faith is both a beacon and a foundation stone. It is born of the Spirit and enriched by a multitude of prayers and promptings. It lifts my soul upwards. It opens my heart to peace and joy. It nourishes and reaffirms those things that I fully know. My faith is such that I know God lives. I know that He lives and Jesus is the Christ and Joseph Smith was a true prophet. May the Lord bless us with faith as we go forward in our lives.

FAITH:
THE FORCE
OF LIFE

Elder Rex D. Pinegar

Not long ago I received a note from a daughter who was leaving home to attend college. After a sweet message of thanks and appreciation, she expressed concern about the responsibilities she would now encounter being on her own. Up until now she felt she had lived a sheltered life and had relied on her family to give her direction and strength. She was beginning to realize that life is hard!

My daughter's note made me think of encounters I've had during the past several months with many members of the Church who seem to be asking, "How do I deal with the difficult challenges of life?"

Life is hard. It is a challenge. At every age life presents trials to bear and difficulties to overcome. Growing up is hard. There are often the heartaches of feeling wronged or rejected. Pursuing an education can press us to our financial, emotional, and intellectual limits. Serving a mission is not easy. It requires total dedication, spiritually and physically. The problems accompanying marriage, rearing a family, earning a living, or coping with illness, old age, and death are realities of life that we are required to meet, but with which we may be unprepared or unwilling to deal.

We will be able to face and solve these challenges more willingly and courageously when we understand that such obstacles are encountered as a natural part of living.

C. S. Lewis wrote: "The great thing, if one can, is to stop regarding all the unpleasant things as interruptions of one's 'own,' or 'real' life. The truth is of course that what one calls the interruptions are precisely one's real life—the life God is sending one day by day." (*They Stand Together: The Letters of C. S. Lewis to Arthur Greeves,* ed. Walter Hooper, London: Collins, 1979, p. 499.)

An old Asian tale describes a prince who was reared in a

castle and kept sheltered from the hardships of life. He never saw anyone who was ill. He never saw anyone who was aged. He never saw anyone die. When the prince grew to be a young man, he desired to go out into the kingdom he ruled. As he was being carried along on a litter, he saw for the first time an old man, toothless, wrinkled, and bent with age.

The prince said to his bearers, "Stop! Wait! What is this?"

The chief bearer replied, "This is a man who is bent with age. Though you are young and strong, the time will come when you too must be bent with age."

This disheartened the prince. His confrontation with aging was more than he could bear. He asked to be taken back to the castle. After a few days in familiar surroundings, he felt rejuvenated. He decided to venture forth again. This time as he passed by a group of men, he noticed that one of them was on the ground, overcome with fever and convulsing in pain.

"What is this?" the prince asked.

"This is a man who is ill," said the porter. "Though you are now young and strong, you too will have to suffer the problems of sickness."

The prince was again saddened, and he returned immediately to the palace. But again in a few days, he wanted to visit his kingdom once more. They hadn't gone far from the castle when the prince saw a coffin being carried to its place of burial.

"What is this?" he asked.

When the meaning of death was explained to the inquiring young prince, he became depressed by the inevitable vision of the future. As he returned to the comfort of his palace, he vowed he would never come out again.

The prince interpreted life to be an evil trick because no matter what a man did or what a man was, he had to suffer sickness, aging, and death.

Perhaps some of us feel about life the way the young prince in this fable did. We may feel that life is cruel and unfair to us, that we would like to retreat into our own shelter and never have to venture forth into the world. To do so, however, would be to deny ourselves the opportunities for growth that life and its experiences are designed to bring to us.

The Lord has made available to us a power that will turn these challenges into opportunities, a power that will enable us to understand the apostle Peter's declaration that such trials of our faith are indeed more precious than gold. (See 1 Peter 1:7.)

When I was teaching an early-morning seminary class a number of years ago, I paused at the end of the year to review some principles we had learned from our study of the Book of Mormon. One young lady held up an illustration in her Book of Mormon, painted by Arnold Friberg. It depicted the two thousand sons of Helaman known as the "stripling soldiers." (See Alma 53:22.) Then in all seriousness she asked, "Tell me, Brother Pinegar, why aren't our young men built like this today?"

Now, I don't know that the young men in the days of the Book of Mormon were built the way Arnold Friberg depicts them, but her question gave me the opportunity to ask, "Where did the *strength* of these young men come from?"

Those who have read the Book of Mormon are familiar with the story of the sons of Helaman. (See Alma 53:56-58.) When their fathers were converted to the gospel, the fathers covenanted with the Lord that they would never again take up arms. But eventually their homes were threatened by hostile armies to the extent that the fathers would have to choose to fight or die. It was then that the two thousand young men, not bound by the same covenant, volunteered to defend their parents and their homes.

A prophet-general described these young men by saying, "They were exceedingly valiant for courage, and also for strength and activity; but behold, this was not all—they were men who were true at all times in whatsoever thing they were entrusted. . . .

"Yea, they had been taught by their mothers, that if they did not doubt, God would deliver them. . . .

"And they . . . fought as if with the strength of God; yea, never were men known to have fought with such miraculous strength; and with such mighty power." (Alma 53:20; 56:47, 56.)

What gave the sons of Helaman their strength? Their faith in God was their "miraculous strength" and "mighty power."

Leo Tolstoy, the famous Russian writer, declared, "Faith is the force of life." Tolstoy had spent the major portion of his life seeking to understand life's purpose. He had found fame, position, fortune. He had married well and had a family. He had experienced success by nearly every measure the world uses. He had sought answers to the meaning of life from his studies of science, philosophy, and other fields of knowledge. However, all the knowledge he had acquired, honors he had received, and personal accomplishments he had achieved brought no lasting satisfaction. Life still seemed to him meaningless. At this point of deepest despair, Tolstoy asked, "How am I to live?" The answer came, "By the Law of God."

Tolstoy was then compelled to admit that "besides the reasoning knowledge," there is "in every living man another kind of knowledge, an unreasoning one, but which gives a possibility of living—faith. . . . Faith is the force of life." (*How I Came to Believe*, Christchurch, New Zealand: The Free Age Press, 1901, p. 40.)

Tolstoy found that one can possess nearly all that one could desire of worldly pleasures and acclaim; but without faith in God, life will burden the heart, the mind, and even the soul.

It sometimes seems that the problems others face are not quite as hard as our own. Some of us may feel that life would not be so hard if we only had more wealth, or if we had a higher social station or better acceptance among our peers. Some may feel that if only they were married, they could be truly happy. Others are seeking to be free from the responsibilities of marriage, thinking *that* would ease their challenges of life.

Not all challenges are related to the presence of a physical or material need. Yet the source of strength to meet all challenges remains the same: faith in God and remaining true at all times. Believing in God and seeking to live His law provides the power to successfully overcome the testing such challenges bring.

A friend of mine from South Carolina has demonstrated that even multiple problems can be overcome when one is true to his faith in God.

Laurie Polk is a dwarf. From the time of his birth, life has been a challenge. When he became old enough to go to school, he pedaled himself on a tricycle in order to move about and keep up with the other children. When his short legs kept him from playing games and participating in athletics, he busied himself in preparing for a vocation in the business world. To obtain employment, he found it necessary to persist and to prove himself. When a job opportunity finally came to him, he found joy in life through his love for his work.

Then another challenge arose. Laurie Polk, already extremely limited in his physical mobility, lost the sight in one eye. Nearly complete loss of the use of his crippled, dwarfed legs followed shortly thereafter. Then, as if that were not enough of a trial for any man, the retina of Laurie's other eye became detached, and complete blindness encompassed him.

Where did Laurie Polk gain his strength to overcome such darkness and despair? Through the power of faith in God, Laurie Polk has learned the meaning of life. In his thirty-four-inch frame, he possesses a strength not unlike the sons of Helaman. Through this strength he not only overcomes the personal challenges he encounters—he actually finds joy in living. He knows he can solve any problem by putting his life in harmony with God and serving his fellow-man. He says, "With the help of the Lord there are no problems, only challenges." Laurie Polk is now a high priest group leader in the Charleston South Carolina Stake.

From my own experience with life's hardships I have

learned that faith in God develops a personal love for Him that is reciprocated through His blessings to us in times of need. To my daughter and to all others who are meeting new or challenging times, I say: Do not fear the challenges of life, but approach them patiently, with faith in God. He will reward your faith with power not only to endure, but also to overcome hardships, disappointments, trials, and struggles of daily living. Through diligently striving to live the law of God and with faith in Him, you will not be diverted from your eternal course either by the ways or the praise of the world.

May each of us develop faith in God sufficient to fight the battles of life victoriously "with the strength of God; yea, . . . with [His] miraculous strength; and . . . mighty power." (Alma 56:56.) We will then find the happiness we so much desire in our lives.

THE FAITH
OF WOMEN

Elder Joseph B. Wirthlin

Women have played a major role in my life. My father labored long hours in his business and in the Church, and for that reason my childhood and teenage years were influenced in a major degree by my mother and my sisters. We have seven daughters and one son. You can see that in our family the girls have the majority, but never have they exercised their majority unrighteously. Our family has had a beautiful spirit of love and consideration one for another. Our son has been kind and considerate of his sisters and his mother. The reason for this wonderful spirit has been the influence of the gospel of Jesus Christ. This spirit fosters the peace that passeth understanding, of which the Savior spoke so beautifully.

My life has been encircled by two special women—my mother, who gave me life itself and who nurtured me in those days when I needed that care, and the girl of my dreams whom I married and who is the loving companion of my life here on this earth and will continue so into the eternities. She has sustained me with an unfailing devotion.

Another important person who taught me a love of this divine Church in my early years was Sister Marion G. Romney, the wife of President Marion G. Romney. She was my Primary teacher who taught me to love and sustain the authorities of the Church and to appreciate the early pioneers who sacrificed so much. President Romney was my coach in those early years and later my bishop, a great leader of youth and of all the Church today.

What are the great principles that women must continually emphasize in their families as mothers and future mothers? First, they should emphasize that God lives, that He is our Creator, that He is interested in each one of us, in our eternal progress and growth. They must teach their sons and daughters to have faith that Jesus is the Christ, the only

Begotten Son of our Heavenly Father, even our Redeemer. Third, they must help their children to possess the faith that Joseph Smith did see God the Father and His Son Jesus Christ, and that he was indeed a true prophet of God. Our sons and daughters must know that it was through Joseph Smith that the gospel, the Church of Jesus Christ, was restored, and that the holy priesthood was given to the Prophet and his associates in order for them to have the power to act for God here upon the earth. And last, they must have the faith to know and realize that they as mothers in our day play a major role in shaping the destiny of their families and the kingdom of God. We must turn this faith into action as did our pioneer ancestry.

One of my grandmothers made great sacrifices for the kingdom of God. My grandfather was called on a mission to Switzerland by President Brigham Young, and without any hesitation he accepted the call. There were three children in the family. They had no money; their only resource was the family cow, and so they sold it in order to provide the traveling expenses for my grandfather. During his mission my grandmother sewed salt sacks for one dollar a thousand in order to sustain her family. She had the faith to endure such tribulation and hardship, to sustain her husband and provide for her three children during the absence of her beloved husband, and also to fulfill her divine calling as a mother.

Another grandmother, Emma Hillstead, was born in Hull, England. Her father and his entire family joined the Church because of a spiritual experience. My grandmother was an extremely spiritual person. She had many dreams that were fulfilled. She loved the Lord and worked diligently to build up the kingdom. When my father left for his mission, she shed tears of joy that her son could be a representative of the Lord in the mission field. She was a Relief Society president during the influenza epidemic following World War I and nursed the sick by day and night. In so doing she weakened her own physical condition, and soon thereafter she passed away.

My maternal grandmother was Martina Halseth, who

was born in Oslo, Norway. As a young girl, Martina loved the Church and its leaders. She was baptized at age fifteen. One weekend when she came downstairs, she heard the elders trying to persuade her parents to give their consent for her to emigrate to America. They would not give it, and so, regardless of their feelings, she joined the group of emigrants who were coming to America and prepared to undertake the journey. Her parents were severely hurt and informed her that she could never come home again if she left. This was no deterrent for this young woman of great faith. Later she learned that all of her family had joined the Church.

Martina endured many hardships crossing the Atlantic ocean. There were 557 souls aboard this sailing ship; 3 adults and 25 children were buried at sea. The water on the ship was so bad that vinegar had to be added to make it drinkable. It took the ship five weeks and six days to cross the ocean. Martina learned as she landed in New York that she had three thousand miles of travel to endure before she could enter the Salt Lake Valley. This news almost overcame her, but she was determined not to give up. When her pioneer group arrived in Quincy, Illinois, they had no shelter for two days during a severe rainstorm. They experienced hardships beyond description during their long trek to the valley. She taxed to the utmost every resource she possessed. One day as she and her girl friend walked a short distance from the camp, Indians attempted to capture them. My grandmother tried to rescue her friend, but an Indian mounted on a horse threw a rope around the other girl and carried her away into captivity. She was never found or heard of again. My grandmother finally reached the valley and in due time married a wonderful man, Brenneman Barr Bitner. They had twelve children, my mother being the twelfth. It was my grandmother's cargo of faith that carried her through her wonderful life, and she bequeathed that same faith to her children.

I do not remember my grandmothers, but one of the most pleasant thoughts for me is to dream of the time that I will meet them in the hereafter and will be able to express my gratitude to them, to those great and mighty women who carried as their cargo in life a great quality of faith in the gospel of Jesus Christ, and bequeathed to us, their children, the teachings of Jesus Christ.

Elder Richard L. Evans said: "A man or a woman must begin to be what he would be, if that's what he wants to be. He must travel the road that leads to the destination he has in mind, if that's where he wants to go. Neither here nor in the hereafter shall we find ourselves becoming overnight something we are not, with qualities we have not earned, nor enjoying a way of life we are not fitted for."

Our sons should never forget the words found in Proverbs: "My son, hear the instruction of thy father, and forsake not the law of thy mother." (Proverbs 1:8.) Remember the words of Paul written to Timothy when he said, "When I call to remembrance the unfeigned faith that is in thee, which dwelt first in thy grandmother Lois, and thy mother Eunice; and I am persuaded that in thee also." (2 Timothy 1:5.)

To the handmaidens of the Lord, Malachi declared in prophetic words, "And they shall be mine, saith the Lord of hosts, in that day when I make up my jewels; and I will spare them, as a man spareth his own son that serveth him." (Malachi 3:17.)

A modern-day prophet, Spencer W. Kimball, has said: "We again ask thy blessing on the women in all the land, that they may accomplish the measure of their creation as daughters of God, thy offspring. Let the blessings of Sarah, Huldah, Hannah, Anna and Mary, the mother of the Son of God bless these women to fulfill their duties as did Mary, the beloved mother of thy Son, and let the power and satisfactions of the prophetesses and all holy women rest upon these mothers as they move forward to fulfill their destinies."

I have faith in the mothers of the kingdom of God that they will uphold the standards, that they will hold high the arms of their sons and their husbands, to the end that the kingdom of God will influence all mankind here upon the earth. May the faith and righteous living of all of us become perfect as we do the will of our Heavenly Father.

FAITH
IN THE LORD
JESUS CHRIST

Elder Gene R. Cook

Someone said long ago that when great events occur, three types of people are manifest: first, the one who doesn't realize that anything great is happening; second, the individual who realizes something is going on but doesn't know what it is; and third, the person behind the scenes making it all happen.

How does a person make things happen? How can someone be effective as a young man or woman, as a father or mother, as a leader in the Church? How can we achieve in school work, at work, in life? I submit that it is by doing things the Lord's way. We can make things happen through faith in the Lord Jesus Christ.

Some are concerned about school work and are unable to perform as well as they would like to. Can faith in the Lord mark the way? Some are worried about employment opportunities. Can faith in the Lord mark the way? Some are concerned about marriage, raising families, sickness, death, personality problems, and personal growth. Once again, can faith in the Lord mark the way?

Some people try to answer difficult questions on their own and hope for the best but still end up making wrong choices. Well might the Lord say to them: "How long will you kick against the pricks? How long will you go along your own way?"

Faithful Latter-day Saints will want to know how to use their faith to cause all things to work for their good (see D&C 90:24), to act and not to be acted upon (see 2 Nephi 2:13-14, 16, 26-27), and to righteously prevail over self and others and situations (see 3 Nephi 7:17-18). They will want to know the specific will of the Lord concerning themselves and then, in faith, discipline themselves to submit to his will.

What is faith? The Prophet Joseph Smith said: "Had it

not been for the principle of faith the worlds would never have been framed neither would man have been formed of the dust. It is the principle by which Jehovah works, and through which he exercises power over all temporal as well as eternal things. Take this principle or attribute—for it is an attribute—from the Diety, and he would cease to exist . . .

"Faith, then, is the first great governing principle which has power, dominion, and authority over all things; by it they exist, by it they are upheld, by it they are changed, or by it they remain, agreeable to the will of God. Without it there is no power, and without power there could be no creation nor existence." (*Lectures on Faith* 1:16, 24.)

The simplest definition I know of faith is "faith is power." How do we exercise faith in order to resolve the challenges of life? How do we learn to use that power to bless ourselves and others? May I offer six specific suggestions.

1. *Be believing.*

How I love these simple but sacred words uttered by Nephi: "I, Nephi, being exceeding young, . . . did cry unto the Lord; and behold He did visit me, and did soften my heart that I did believe all the words which had been spoken by my father; wherefore, I did not rebel against him like unto my brothers." (1 Nephi 2:16.)

Are you believing? Are you able to exercise faith in the words of your parents and leaders with little or no tangible evidence? Remember that unbelief destroys faith. We learn this about unbelieving Laman and Lemuel. "Laman was angry with me, and also with my father; and also was Lemuel, for he hearkened unto the words of Laman." (1 Nephi 3:28.)

Some people are confused or deceived and follow strange voices such as Laman's. They believe in unworthy causes or men or embrace untrue principles. Nephi taught his brethren how one receives most communication from God: "He hath spoken unto you in a still small voice, but ye were past feeling, that ye could not feel his words." (1 Nephi 17:45.)

How much evidence do you require before you are able to act in faith? Are you capable of believing the inspired words of others or only your own experience? Faith cannot be based on physical evidence. You must first exercise your faith, and signs will follow. You will receive spiritual evidence as you go forth believing.

2. *Commit yourself.*

For many persons it is harder to make a true commitment than to actually fulfill what the commitment requires. Such individuals may go through life allowing life to serve up the menu. They seem to be subject to every wind of doctrine and mood of the world. They go forth lost in the world with only a vague idea of what they would have from life.

Others decide what they want, commit themselves to obtain it, and, in righteousness, exercise their faith until they do so. They keep spiritual priorities ever present in their minds and hearts until they have reached that which they righteously desire. Once again, Nephi's sacred commitment and personal discipline in this respect greatly moves me. He said: "As the Lord liveth, and as we live, we will not go down unto our father in the wilderness until we have accomplished the thing which the Lord hath commanded us." (1 Nephi 3:15.)

Faith in the Lord Jesus Christ is fully sustaining. You can cause things to happen by disciplining yourself and paying the price. Hold your word as sacred to God and man. Be truly committed, and you will see the hand of the Lord revealed in your behalf.

Let me tell you of a young man I knew when I was a mission president. A Uruguayan, he had been in the mission about three or four months when I arrived, and I noticed that wherever he served, people were being baptized. In the beginning I thought it was because of his senior companion, because he seemed too young, too new, to be the cause. That was my mistake. He knew how to make things happen.

He was called as a senior companion and a district leader. I sent him into a city that had gained a reputation of being a tough, no-results city. Missionaries had not baptized anyone there for nearly a year—not one person. The members were discouraged. Only ten to twelve persons were attending the branch. I didn't tell the missionary anything—I just notified him of the transfer. Three weeks later, he and his companion began baptizing. He served there about ten weeks. All of his district started baptizing. It is great to have a missionary who can baptize, but if he can teach others how to do it, his leadership can bless the lives of many.

This missionary never wrote me much in his weekly reports. He would only write, "Dear President, I sure love you. Things are going great. Sincerely," or "President, the Lord is blessing us greatly. I love the work. Your brother."

He was called later to serve as a zone leader and was sent to supervise the whole upper area of the mission where there were some very challenging cities. His new challenge was to teach the missionaries to do what he was doing. He served there two or three months and was responsible for scores of baptisms. He literally changed the spirit of the whole zone, member leaders as well as missionaries. Together they wrought a spiritual miracle.

Then came a spiritual struggle for me, a restless feeling about him. I felt impressed that he should be sent to Paraguay. At that time the work was very slow in Paraguay. We averaged only twenty to twenty-five baptisms a month in the whole country. I wrestled with that and thought to myself, *He has really proved himself here, but to put him in that situation might drag him down in discouragement as it has so many others. He may have a hard time sustaining his faith there.* I had to struggle with my faith to convince myself that he really ought to go, but I obeyed the promptings.

I sent him a telegram transferring him to Asunción, Paraguay, as a zone leader and told him that he should leave the very next day. When he came into Montevideo, he didn't even come to see me. He was modest and always a little embarrassed to see "the president." When he departed from the mission home, he left a letter, the first one I had ever received from him. It said, in effect, "Dear President Cook, I received a telegram today telling me to go to Paraguay, and I thought you ought to know a few things: (1) You can't baptize in Paraguay. I have had at least ten to fifteen elders tell me of their experiences there. (2) The members are not helping at all. (3) There are some real morality problems among the nonmembers there. (4) Many people live together unmarried. (5), (6), (7), (8) . . ." And he went through and listed ten to twelve of some of the most negative things that I have ever heard in my life.

I thought to myself, *Oh, no, unbelieving people have gotten to him.*

But at the end of the list, he wrote, "I just wanted you to know, President, that I don't believe any of those things." Talk about faith! Then, after expressing his faith, he committed himself, saying, "I want you to know, President Cook, that on Christmas Day [the date of the letter was December 1], we are going to baptize twenty-five people."

When I read that, I prayed for him and thought, *The Lord bless you, elder. You have a tremendous amount of faith, and the Lord will sustain you. You don't know the country; you haven't ever been there. You don't know where you are going to live. You don't know your companion, the leaders, the members. You don't know anything, and yet you, in faith, believe that you are going to baptize twenty-five people in twenty-five days.*

Well, this young man was full of faith and was a real example of a great Latin leader. On December 25, he and his companion baptized eighteen people. They hadn't reached the twenty-five, but eighteen was just about all that the whole country baptized in a normal month. It was a great privilege two weeks later to participate in a baptismal service where he and his companion baptized eleven more. His district baptized about thirty that day. Can you see how one righteous man can turn around a whole set of circumstances? He believed, he committed, and he and the Lord did it.

You too can literally cause things to work for your good both in your life and in the lives of others if you are full of faith in the Lord. "All things are possible to him that believeth." (Mark 9:23.) Commit yourself in advance to what you righteously desire. The righteous exercising of faith will bring it about.

3. *Do your part.*

People falter and expect the Lord to do more than His part. It is evident in all of scripture that unless a person does do all in his power, the arm of the Lord will not be revealed in his behalf. After one has truly sacrificed and done all in his power, God will come and save him in his time of need. As James taught us, "By works was faith made perfect." (James 2:22.)

We must not only pay the price the Lord requires, but also search to understand in what currency it will be required. The sacrifice most often required by the Lord is our own personal sins. He desires us to sacrifice those to Him and obtain the broken heart and contrite spirit that He requires of all persons.

Do all in your power to do your part.

4. *Pray.*

Pray as if all depended upon the Lord. Will He not honor the sacrifice of His servants if they will ask it of Him? Sometimes people arrive at this point and do not actually come to ask Him for the gift of faith or for power in the priesthood. The Lord taught, "Ask, and ye shall receive; knock, and it shall be opened unto you." (D&C 4:7.)

The initiative rests with us. The Lord said, "It should be granted unto them according to their faith in their prayers." (D&C 10:47.)

If we exercise great faith in our prayers and fasts as needed, our loving, all-knowing Father will provide all with what we righteously desire. Pray, believing you will have your righteous desires, and they will, in the Lord's time, be given to you.

5. *Expect trials of your faith.*

Tribulation is a refiner of faith. The Lord said, "For after much tribulation come the blessings." (D&C 58:4.)

The Lord will never tempt a person, but He will try him. Tribulations and problems are what this earthly school is made of. Life is all upstream—all uphill. One may at times desire to remove himself from the swift current to rest awhile, but he must go on. Some persons are on plateaus and need to be on their way. They are not praying fervently and receiving trials in the right spirit.

The challenges and difficulties that many of us resist are the very elements that refine us and make us godly. The Lord will try us in every attribute possessed by man and at all stages of development in our lives. He will try us again and again and again until we know that we will serve Him at all costs.

How comforting the words of Moroni: "I would show unto the world that faith is things which are hoped for and not seen; wherefore, dispute not because ye see not, for ye receive no witness until after the trial of your faith." (Ether 12:6.)

6. *Expect the Lord to act.*

We must expect the Lord to perform according to His holy will and our faith. His arm will be revealed. He will take care of His Saints. He wants other people to learn faith by our example. He wants us to cause things to happen. He wants us to draw upon His all-powerful arm and the power that resides in us to do things in His way. He desires us not to be too deeply involved in or absorbed by worldly, temporal, superficial, or secondary things. These things must be dealt with, but even they must be handled spiritually.

When we pray for something that does not occur the way we desire it to, we must not lose faith. In the Lord's own way and time, all righteous prayers are answered, but His way and His time may not be the same as ours. Sometimes when a prayer appears to go unanswered, it is because it is being answered in a greater way than we can perceive. When we face these trials, we must double our faith lest we lose it.

Be sure to receive with a thankful heart whatever the Lord gives you. Alma said, "There are some among you who would humble themselves, let them be in whatsoever circumstances they might." (Alma 32:25.) The same could be said of those who have a thankful heart: There are some among you who would have a thankful heart; let them be in whatsoever circumstances they might.

Remember the heartfelt response of Job after losing all he

possessed. He said, "The Lord gave, and the Lord hath taken away; blessed be the name of the Lord." (Job 1:21.)

Be submissive, humble, and patient, and the Lord will deliver to you that which will be for your good.

I would like now to relate one last personal experience in faith that demonstrates these six suggestions.

On July 29, 1977, Sister Cook and I had just finished visiting the Bolivia Santa Cruz Mission and were stalled in the airport at Cochabamba, Bolivia, for some five hours. I recall that we were very tired, having had few hours of sleep the night before. We were both delighted to have a few hours rest in the airport. As I was drifting off to sleep, I had a very strong feeling that I should awaken and write down some ideas. The desire to sleep was strong, but the promptings of the Spirit were more powerful. I did write; in fact, I wrote for nearly three hours, solving some organizational problems I had struggled with for a number of years previously. I felt a great outpouring of the Spirit on that day and excitedly wrote down each inspired thought. The experience took most of the time of the delay.

We were then off to La Paz, Bolivia. We were graciously met by President and Sister Chase Allred at the airport and driven in their van to the mission office. We locked the car and left our luggage and briefcase in the van.

Upon entering the office, the president was confronted with the difficult case of a woman whose husband was dying. While President Allred and I assisted with her needs, Sisters Cook and Allred left for the mission home.

When the president and I returned to the van, I realized immediately that all of our goods were gone but assumed that Sister Cook had taken them with her to the mission home. While we were driving toward the home, I discovered that the right front window-wing had been damaged, and I began to fear that our goods had been stolen.

Arriving at the mission home, we found that our luggage had indeed been stolen. The loss of a substantial amount of money and all our clothing created an immediate but only temporary problem. More disheartening was the fact that my scriptures were in my briefcase along with the inspired ideas I had just received in Cochabamba. The sensation of discouragement, anger, and inability to do anything about the situation was overpowering.

My wife and I prayed alone. We prayed with those present. We tried to enjoy our dinner but could not. Who could know of the great loss I personally felt? The scriptures had been given to me as a young man by my parents, a sacred inscription placed in one of them by my mother and in the other by my since-deceased father. I had spent literally thousands of hours marking and cross-referencing (and loving every moment of it) in the only tangible earthly possessions I had ever considered of much value. I had on many occasions instructed my wife that if there were ever a fire in the home, she should first remove the children and then, if there were time, save my scriptures and not worry about anything else.

The president and I had much to discuss, as we were to be together only that evening. However, I felt a strong impression that we must do all in our power to recover the scriptures. After supper, all present knelt in prayer once again. We determined to search the immediate area near the mission office and in a nearby field, hoping that the thief or thieves had taken the salable items and discarded the English books.

In the prayer we pleaded that the scriptures would be returned, that the persons who had taken them would be led to know of their unrighteous act and repent, and that the return of the books would be the means of bringing someone into the true church.

Eight to ten of us then loaded into the van with flashlights and warm clothing and drove up to the mission office in the central city. We scoured vacant lots across the street and adjacent streets and alleys; we talked with guards and anyone else we could find, and exhausted all possibilities. No one had seen or heard anything. Finally we returned home, dejected, able only to pray individually and wait. President Allred and I worked late into the night to finish our business, and the next day Sister Cook and I flew back to Quito, Ecuador, where we lived.

During the next few weeks, the missionaries searched the lots again. They looked in hedges and garbage cans, searched a nearby park, placed a sign on a wall near where the books were stolen, requesting their return, and kept a watchful eye to see if the books might show up in an unexpected place nearby. In sheer desperation, the missionaries decided to place an ad in two daily newspapers, offering a reward and giving explicit information concerning the books.

In Quito, Ecuador, I began a personal spiritual struggle that was a very difficult one for me. After nearly three weeks, I had not studied the scriptures at all. I had tried on numerous occasions, but every time I read a verse, I recalled only a few of the many cross-references I had made over twenty years. I was disheartened, depressed, and had no desire whatsoever to read. I prayed many times expressing to the Father that I had never tried to use my scriptures for any purpose other than to glorify His name and try to teach others the truths that He had taught me. I pleaded with Him to do whatever had to be done in order to have them returned. My wife and little children prayed incessantly for the same blessing. Even after two or three weeks they continued praying every day, "Heavenly Father, please bring back Daddy's scriptures."

After about three weeks, I felt a strong spiritual impression, "Elder Cook, how long will you go on without reading and studying?" It seemed to me to be a test or a trial and to have something to do with the cost of the blessing I desired. The words burned, and I determined that I must be humble and submissive enough to start all over again. With my wife's permission to use her scriptures, I began reading in Genesis in the Old Testament, marking and cross-referencing once again.

On August 18, a friend, Brother Ebbie Davis, arrived in Ecuador from Bolivia and laid my scriptures on my desk along with a manila folder that contained the papers I had written in Cochabamba and some recently prepared mission budgets that were also stolen. He indicated that they were the only things recovered, that he had been given those items by the mission president in La Paz as he boarded the plane, and that he did not know how the books were found, but that I would be told when I arrived there in the next few days to tour the mission.

The joy I experienced in that moment and later that day is indescribable. To realize that my Heavenly Father could, in some miraculous way, lift those books out of the hands of thieves in a city like La Paz and return them intact, not one page removed, torn, or soiled, is still beyond me. How the faith of our family and many Bolivian missionaries was rewarded! That day I promised my Father that I would make better use of my scriptures and my time as instruments in His hands for teaching the gospel.

On Sunday, August 21, I flew to Guayaquil, Ecuador, and on to La Paz, Bolivia, arriving on August 22. Upon arrival I was given the following account:

A woman in one of La Paz's hundreds of marketplaces saw a drunk man waving a black book around. She had the strongest spiritual impression that something holy was being desecrated. She approached the man and asked him what it was. He did not know but showed her the book. She asked if he had anything else. He pulled out another black book. She asked if there were more. He removed a folder full of papers that he said he was going to burn. She then expressed a desire to purchase those things from him, to which he agreed, for the price of 50 pesos or about $2.50, U.S. currency.

After the purchase had been made, she felt totally taken back by what she had done. She realized the books and papers were in English—she didn't speak, read, or understand English—and she had no desire to have any English books. It would have been like one of us paying nearly ten percent of our monthly income to buy some books in a language we could not read. She immediately began a search for the church that was named in the front of the books. After approaching a number of other churches, she finally arrived at the mission office in La Paz, directed by the hand of the Lord.

She had never heard of the reward nor of the ad in the newspaper, which was to appear that very day. She did not ask for any money, not even to reclaim the 50 pesos that she had paid for the books and papers. The elders received the books with rejoicing and paid her the reward anyway.

She told the missionaries that she was associated with a Pentecostal sect, but she listened very intently as they unfolded the gospel to her. She recalled reading something about Joseph Smith from a pamphlet she had picked up in the street two or three years earlier. After their first discussion with her, they reported, "She is a golden contact." After the second discussion, she committed to baptism. Two weeks later, on Sunday, September 11, 1977, in La Paz, Bolivia, Sister Maria Cloefe Cardenas Terrazas and her son, Marco Fernando Miranda Cardenas, age twelve, were baptized into the true church of Jesus Christ by Elder Douglas Reeder.

Who could describe my deep, discouraging, depressing, disheartening, overpowering feelings of helplessness when the scriptures were lost? Who could describe my great feelings of joy and rejoicing when we saw the power of heaven revealed in this miraculous way?

Our Heavenly Father does hear and answer the prayers of His sons and daughters if they exercise faith in the Lord Jesus Christ. The Lord said: "For verily I say unto you, That whosoever shall say unto this mountain, Be thou removed, and be thou cast into the sea; and shall not doubt in his heart, but shall believe that those things which he saith shall come to pass; he shall have whatsoever he saith. Therefore I say unto you, What things soever ye desire, when ye pray, believe that ye receive them, and ye shall have them." (Mark 11:23-24.)

Today is a day of miracles. We believe in miracles. The Latter-day Saints may expect miracles according to their faith. As a member of the Church, you are authorized to take a leading part in the development of the kingdom of God on earth within your respective responsibilities. Pray fervently. Actively seek to increase your faith, and with that great gift from God, you can cause great things to occur within your life and in the lives of others.

May the Lord bless you that that responsibility may rest squarely upon you. Remember, faith in the Lord Jesus Christ is fully sustaining. Will the Lord mark the way in your schooling, in your employment, in your marriage, in your family? He will. The Lord is full of mercy, forgiveness, patience, and long-suffering and is desirous of unlocking His treasure house of blessings to all who are full of faith.

WE KNOW
THROUGH FAITH

Elder F. Enzio Busche

The Spirit of God touches our hearts with the assurance that we human beings are children of a loving Father in heaven and that Jesus is the Christ, the Savior of mankind. Through the power of that Spirit, we know that we are born free; and because of this free agency, we know that we are responsible for all our actions, words, and thoughts, and that some day we will be held accountable for them by our Father in heaven. As members of The Church of Jesus Christ of Latter-day Saints, we know that He wants us to come to him every day to pour out our hearts before Him, to constantly ask Him for our needs, and to confess that we will do all we can in faith, that our life and the life of our neighbor, of our family, and of society will be improved daily. As members of His church, we have been charged to proclaim to all people not to procrastinate the day of repentance. In the Book of Mormon we read, "For behold, this life is the time for men to prepare to meet God; yea, behold the day of this life is the day for men to perform their labors . . . For that same spirit which doth possess your bodies at the time ye go out of this life, . . . will have power to possess your body in that eternal world." (Alma 34: 32-34.)

How happy we are to be able to increase our knowledge daily through study, prayer, and service in obedience to His laws and commandments so that our love, faith, and hope can continue to grow. Our faith can become as strong as Nephi's, the descendant of Helaman, of whom is said in the Book of Mormon, "So great was his faith on the Lord Jesus Christ that angels did minister to him daily. And in the name of Jesus did he cast out devils and unclean spirits; and even his brother did he raise from the dead, after he had been stoned and suffered death by the people." (3 Nephi 7:18-19.)

We read in Matthew, "If ye have faith as a grain of mustard seed, ye shall say unto this mountain, Remove hence to yonder place; and it shall remove; and nothing shall be impossible unto you." (Matthew 17:20.) A grain of mustard, no matter how small, has the strength to trust that, if it is cared for and put in the ground, it will be able to grow to the size of a big tree and bear good fruit.

As we look around, we discover a great variety of human beings, every one precious, a jewel in his own way. Man is waiting to be discovered, promoted, and touched until his inner potential can be realized. No one is inferior; no one is unimportant; no one is rejected under the careful attention of the servants of the Lord through the priesthood in His true church. Under the influence of the spoken word and the eternal light and the manifestation of the Holy Ghost, man grows to an unknown height. Nothing is impossible to him who believes.

The Savior said, "Come unto me, all ye that labour and are heavy laden, and I will give you rest." (Matthew 11:28.) How does He give us rest? He touches our soul and opens our eyes so that we may perceive the purpose of life through His love for each and every one of us, if through faith we humbly seek him in prayer. He also gives us rest through His church, which is completely organized and is led by a living prophet. Therefore, we are not left alone in our knowledge and understanding. The Church is an organization that in its far-reaching purposes, is destined to fill the basic needs of men for love, dignity, growth, and joy, even for salvation and exaltation through the law of service and love for one another.

What joy it is to be allowed to take upon oneself the yoke of Jesus Christ in His church and thereby escape the trouble and anxiety of this world. The greatest commandment, "Thou shalt love thy neighbour as thyself" (Leviticus 19:18), is attainable through communion with the Spirit of God and mutual participation in service to one another. Because of His mercy, we are daily facing new tasks and are permitted to be called to special service in His church. I am convinced that whoever will draw near unto the Lord Jesus Christ in all his decisions in faith and prayer will have his life filled with more light and joy.

Not long ago I had an experience that brought me particularly close to our Savior. I had a conversation with someone from another denomination. He talked about his work, his faith, and his conviction. I felt a relationship and love when I could testify to him that the true church has been restored in these latter days through the Prophet Joseph Smith. This man seemed like a brother to me in his straightforwardness, and I thought I might learn something from him. But then something happened. The more my love and my ability to listen to him as a brother increased, the more his disposition changed. The expression on his face became braced and clenched. His words expressed harshness and indifference. He could not stand to listen any longer. When we separated, I thought I noticed fear in his eyes and hatred as a result of it.

The Savior met this same kind of hatred while He lived on this earth. Although He was pure and His love was perfect, only those who recognized Him had sufficient faith to give up everything in their search for perfection. The Lord in His boundless love shows us what He had to go through when He walked the earth and testified of the truth.

Truth cannot be divided; we cannot get away from it. It was impenitent men who could not tolerate Christ and His teachings because of their hatred and fear. They had to cover up their ears when he spoke. Finally they persecuted and killed him. Nevertheless, His death was the final victory, the victory of immortality over mortality, the victory of light over darkness. We are witnesses of the crucified Christ and of His resurrection. We call upon all men with good intentions to get to know Him in His church, restored in these latter days by the Prophet Joseph Smith. We call upon mankind to change its ways and to accept the importance of a clean life, to draw closer unto the Lord through study, work, diligence, faith, and prayer, and to become aware that all yearning of men is the yearning for the light of the gospel of Jesus Christ, which is the only source of real joy.

MAN'S ETERNAL HORIZON

Elder Joseph Anderson

It has been truly said that the greatest asset of a man or a nation is faith, that the men who built America and made it prosper during its darkest days were men with unshakable faith, men of courage, men of vision, men who always looked forward and never backward.

The same can be said in truth of those who established the Church under the inspiration and revelation of the Lord and of those who have built upon the foundation they laid. They too were and are men of unfailing testimony and unwavering faith.

There has never been greater need for faith than is the need today, particularly faith in divine leadership. Members of The Church of Jesus Christ of Latter-day Saints, as a general rule, have faith in divine leadership, but the world needs faith in God, that He rules the world.

Many of us have had the experience of being on a ship traveling on the ocean. As we look in the various directions, we can see nothing but water. As far as the mortal eye can see, the sky comes down and meets the water. The sun comes up on the horizon, and in the evening the sun sets on the horizon. The same is true when we are on the ground: the limit of our vision is the horizon. Is it not true also that the limit of our spiritual perception is the horizon we see?

What about our spiritual horizon? Is it limited to our present struggle for the things of this world? Is it limited to an acquisition of things of the flesh? Is it limited to our competition with a money-mad world, to the obtaining of the worldly things of life, or does it reach out to an eternity with God and our loved ones in the life to come?

Our horizon should extend to an unlimited future beyond death—out beyond those things of a temporal nature. Our horizon of the future should not be confused with the close-up horizon of present conditions.

Our philosophy of life contemplates an eternity of life—life without beginning before we came here, life without end hereafter. Our happiness here and hereafter depends upon our actions here. We should therefore seek the finer things of life. The road leading to eternal life must be paved with obedience to the commandments of the Lord.

We once dwelt in the presence of our Father, in the spirit, and we rejoiced at the opportunity to come to earth, take upon ourselves mortality, and pass through the experiences we here encounter, that we might prove ourselves worthy of greater experiences and greater blessings.

While we are here, we are not to enjoy the presence of our Father, but we can communicate with Him, and we can hear His voice if that becomes necessary. The Holy Ghost is given to us as our guide and companion and monitor, if we live worthy of that blessing.

It seems difficult for some to have faith in an eternal being and faith that He can communicate with man; that He hears and answers our prayers; that He is the Father of our spirits, for we are dual beings, spiritual and physical; that He loves us; and that He has given us commandments which, if we accept and live them, will result in mortal as well as eternal blessings to us.

There was a time when men would have laughed to scorn anyone who said that in time to come we would be able to sit in our own homes and watch and see and hear things that were transpiring in our own country, in Europe or Asia, South America or Africa. In our time we have seen men walk on the moon, heard the messages they have sent over the great expanse of space between us and the moon, and witnessed pictures they were transmitting. These things have been accomplished by faith, by work, and by intelligence.

Can we talk with God?

Can our prayers, in thought as well as word, ascend to the Father of us all, and does He have the power to answer them?

We lived by sight in the spirit state before we came here;

we are walking by faith in this mortal existence. The Spirit of God bears witness to the spirit of man that we are God's children; that He loves us; that there is a purpose to earth life, a great and mighty purpose, a glorious purpose; that by keeping the commandments that He has given us, we may gain knowledge and understanding; that we may gain experience by overcoming the opposition with which we must contend; that we shall resurrect from the grave in the due time of the Lord and eventually return into His presence if we live worthily. This is the long-distance horizon we should keep in view.

Alma, a Book of Mormon prophet, related an experience in his time about a people who were cast out of the synagogues because of the coarseness of their apparel, a people who were poor as to the things of this world and were also poor in heart. They came unto Alma, explained their situation, and asked what they should do. Alma answered by explaining to them the principle of faith and teaching them the word of God. Concerning faith he stated that "faith is not to have a perfect knowledge of things; therefore if ye have faith ye hope for things which are not seen, which are true." (Alma 32:21.)

Alma then went on to compare his words, which are truly the word of God and the gospel of salvation, to a seed that a man plants in the soil. He suggested that if one will give place that a seed may be planted in his heart, and not cast it out or resist the Spirit of the Lord, if it is a true seed it will swell within the breast. When one feels this swelling motion, he cannot do otherwise than admit that the seed is a good seed, for it enlarges the soul and begins to enlighten one's understanding, and it becomes delicious to the individual. Further, when the seed, or the word, or the gospel, swells and sprouts and begins to grow in one's soul, he knows it is a good seed, and therefore his knowledge is perfect. It is no longer faith but knowledge.

People sometimes say that one cannot know that the gospel is true. As indicated by Alma, if, when we hear the word of God, we do not cast it out by unbelief or resist the Spirit of the Lord, the swellings within our breast, its enlargement of our soul, and its enlightening of our understanding are of such a nature that they cause us to know that it is the truth.

However, this is only a beginning. We must nourish the seed; in other words, we must nourish the testimony we have that it is true, by living the teachings of the gospel.

If we will do this, this ancient prophet said, the seed will grow into a tree and bring forth fruit. But if the tree is neglected, it will not take root; and when the heat of the sun cometh and scorcheth it, it will wither and die. This is not because the seed or the word of God was not true nor because the fruit thereof would not be desirable, but because the ground was barren and the plant or the tree was not nourished, in which event we cannot have the fruit thereof that we otherwise would obtain.

If, however, we have faith and patience to nourish the word, or the tree, as time goes on we may pluck the fruit thereof, which is most precious and delicious to the taste. We shall have the privilege of feasting upon this fruit, and our faith will be fully rewarded and will develop into a sure knowledge of the truth of the gospel of Jesus Christ.

The Latter-day Saints believe and teach that without the experience of mortal life, its problems and accomplishments, and without a resurrected body, the spirit of man cannot have a fulness of joy. Our philosophy of life contemplates an eternity of existence—life without beginning in the preexistent world and life hereafter throughout the eternities.

Our happiness in this life and in the life to come depends upon our actions here. If we are to attain the goal of eternal salvation and exaltation in the kingdom of our Heavenly Father, we must hold fast to the iron rod, which is the word of God, and render obedience to the commandments of the Lord.

It is reported that on one occasion when Sir Isaac Newton was thinking seriously concerning the nature of light, he cut a hole in a window blind and a ray of light entered his room. He held a triangular piece of glass in the range of the light, and there, reflected in great beauty, were all the colors of the rainbow. For the first time, man learned that all of the glorious colors of the universe are locked up in a ray of white light.

It is important that we live all the principles of the gospel and obey all the commandments the Lord has given us if we are to grow more nearly like our Father and his Beloved Son. We cannot say, "Oh, I believe in missionary work—it is important; I am thoroughly converted to the welfare plan or the wonderful social program of the Church for its young people; but I don't believe that Joseph Smith was a prophet or that our present prophets are guided by revelation from the Lord."

Some may say, "I believe the Book of Mormon, but I can't believe that it was received from an angel as Joseph said it was."

With wavering faith of that kind, how can such a person expect to have the true light of Christ, the true understanding and light of the gospel? How can he expect to receive the blessings that the Lord has promised to the faithful? If he leaves out any one of these principles, he does not receive pure white light. If he fails to have faith in all the principles of the gospel and does not have faith to live in accordance therewith, he cannot expect to get the pure light of the gospel in his heart.

If we truly have faith in God sufficient to impel us to keep His commandments, we will draw nearer to Him and He will come nearer to us. Our faith will become knowledge, and the limit of our horizon will extend into the eternal world.

May we grow in faith through the love and blessing of our Lord and Savior. May we keep the commandments that he has given us, that we may ultimately find salvation and exaltation in his celestial kingdom.

INDEX

Ability, faith as: to recognize Lord as all powerful, 80-81; to follow spiritual promptings, 81-82; to live commandments, 82; to act "as if," 82-83; to be charitable, 83; to follow priesthood, 83-85
Abraham, 3-5, 8
Adams, John, 23-24
Adams, Samuel, 24
Adversity, 50-51
Aging, 87
Allred, Chase, 103-4
Alma, 114
Apostles to rely on Holy Ghost, 31-32
Ark of Noah, 3, 8
Armor of God, 60-61
Assurance from faith, 64
Attitude, proper, from faith, 49-53
Attributes of God, 57-58

Belief, 14-19, 34-35, 39, 83, 97-98
Believing is seeing, 43
Birth of Jesus Christ, 16
Bitner, Brenneman Barr, 94
Blessing of son, 81-82
Blessings from faith, 81-82
Blind man, example of, 70-71
Bolivia, loss of scriptures in, 103-7

Cardenas, Marco, 107
Challenges, facing: unavoidability of, 86-88; faith in, 88-91
Character of God, 57-58
Children, faith of, 40-41
Clark, J. Reuben, Jr., 22-23
Colors, learning, 76
Comforter, Jesus Christ as, 16-17
Commager, Henry Steele, 22
Commandments, keeping, 82
Commitment, 98-100
Communication with God, 113
Cornfield, miracle of, 72-74
Cowdery, Oliver, 2
Crabb, Nolan, 70-71
Creation, 15

Davis, Ebbie, 105-6
Death, 87
Decalogue, 15
Decisions, 65-66
Declaration of Independence, 21, 24-25
DeHaan, Douglas W. 72-74
Determination, 50-51
Dwarf, example of, 90-91

Elijah, 6-8
Error, distinguishing truth from, 10-12
Evans, Richard L., 95
Evidence, demonstrative, 36-37
Expectations about Lord, 102-3
Experience, faith from, 42-43

Faith: witness and miracles follow, 1-2, 7-9, 55-56, 67-68; is not developed by miracles, 2-3; examples of, preceding miracles, 3-7, 54; power of, 10-13, 54-55, 96-97; in Jesus Christ, 14-19, 96, 108; of Founding Fathers, 20-25, 112; United States must rely on, 25-27; of prophets, 28-33; in Christ from asking God, 34-35; in Christ is first step, 36-39; nature and need of, 37; seed of, 37-38, 56, 59, 114-15; of children, 40-41; of brother of Jared, 41-42; nature of, 42-44, 64-66, 80, 96-97; in oneself, 45-49; personality traits from, 49-53; fruits of, 54-56; increasing, 56-59; shield of, 60-61; examples of persons of, 62-64, 68-71, 74-75; in saving stake farm, 72-74; secular learning and, 77-79; as ability to do things, 80-85; to face challenges, 86-91; of women, 92-95; exercising, by belief, 97-98; exercising, by commitment, 98-100; exercising, by doing our part, 101; exercising, by prayer, 101; exercising, by expecting trials, 101-2; exercising, by expecting Lord to act, 102-3; example of, in loss of scriptures, 103-7; knowledge

117